Tally's Blood

Ann Marie Di Mambro

HODDER
GIBSON
AN HACHETTE UK COMPANY

Acknowledgements

Hachette UK's policy is to use papers that are natural, renewable and recyclable products and made from wood grown in sustainable forests. The logging and manufacturing processes are expected to conform to the environmental regulations of the country of origin.

Orders: please contact Bookpoint Ltd, 130 Park Drive, Milton Park, Abingdon, Oxon OX14 4SE. Telephone: (44) 01235 827720. Fax: (44) 01235 400454. Lines are open 9.00-5.00, Monday to Saturday, with a 24-hour message answering service. Visit our website at www.hoddereducation.co.uk. Hodder Gibson can be contracted direct on: Tel: 0141 333 4650; Fax: 0141 404 8188; email: hoddergibson@hodder.co.uk

The right of Ann Marie Di Mambro to be identified as the author of this work has been asserted by her in accordance with the Copyright, Designs and Patents Act 1988.

First published by Learning and Teaching Scotland in 2002 and subsequently by Education Scotland.

This edition Ann Marie Di Mambro 2014

This edition first published in 2014 by

Hodder Gibson, an imprint of Hodder Education,

An Hachette UK Company

211 St Vincent Street

Glasgow G2 5QY

Impression number   6

Year   2018 2017

Cover image courtesy of the Traverse Theatre; photographs property of the author

Typeset in ITC Legacy Serif Book 12/14 by Datapage (India) Pvt. Ltd

Printed and bound by CPI Group (UK) Ltd, Croydon, CR0 4YY

A catalogue record for this title is available from the British Library

ISBN: 978 1 4718 08401

Contents

Introduction

A piece of advice: If you're reading this text for the first time, you might want to save reading the Introduction until after you've finished the play. There are a few plot spoilers below, which the author wouldn't want to taint your experience of the play as a whole.

Tally's Blood was first performed at the Traverse Theatre, Edinburgh, in 1990. So much has changed since then. We've got mobile phones, social networks, Google, YouTube and a seemingly infinite number of apps. We have never had so much access to drama. We can watch an entire television series on demand or download two-minute dramas onto our mobiles.

So why are we still going to the theatre?

What does a theatre play give us that we can't get elsewhere? I think the answer is *uninterrupted drama*. It is happening before our eyes and we can't pause it to answer the phone. We can't change channels. We can't Tweet about it while it's on. A theatre play demands our full attention.

A theatre play demands that we understand the characters and the world they inhabit. The world I chose for *Tally's Blood* was that of Italian immigrants before, during and after the Second World War. The Italian immigrant experience is one I know well from my own background. I was born in Scotland to Italian parents and was brought up with an awareness of my Italian identity and with stories of what happened to Italians in Scotland during the war. I frequently resented my Italian upbringing and the ways in which it stopped me fitting in with my peers. I had very loving parents but I wasn't allowed to go to dance halls or to coffee bars (where the cool kids hung out in my day). I wasn't allowed out with boys until I was seventeen. We were told that being Italian meant a stronger sense of family.

All of this influenced the characters of Rosinella and Franco, as well as Lucia, Hughie and Bridget. Franco kicks against his Italian identity to such an extent that he signs up to the British army and subsequently gets killed. When Lucia grows up, Rosinella drums it into her that being Italian makes her special and she can't be allowed to do what other girls her age are allowed to do. Rosinella is fond of Hughie but looks down on his family. When she realises that he and Lucia have feelings for each other she is horrified, and is mean and spiteful to and about Hughie.

I always think of Rosinella as the stereotypical warm Italian mamma – but without the children. Her inability to have a child is a deep-rooted pain which she carries. As a writer, I find it very useful to ask this question of my characters: *What do they want?* Very simply, Rosinella wants to be a mother.

For me, the theme of motherhood runs deeply through the play and really informs the character of Rosinella. Lucia gives Rosinella the chance to be a mother. But it's worth asking whether she is a good mother. She is resentful of Bridget and Hughie's mother and her eight children because she feels that it is her right, as an Italian, to be the mother of a large brood.

Another useful question I ask of my characters is: *What is the worst thing that could happen to them?* For Rosinella I thought at first it was losing Lucia. And this is what happens. Lucia is called back to Italy by her father and Rosinella is bereft, consumed by her own pain. But there is worse to come. She finds out that not only did Bridget abort Franco's baby, but she did it because of what Rosinella told her and how she treated her. In short, Rosinella is made to feel responsible for the loss of Franco's baby. This is the antithesis of motherhood and possibly Rosinella's darkest moment. To me, this is worse for Rosinella than losing Lucia and is a very bitter blow.

But there is still one more body blow to come. For most of the play Massimo is a loving, hard-working husband. Rosinella has taken centre stage in this marriage and, though he finds her quite high maintenance, Massimo loves her.

But when she is at her lowest ebb he finally confronts her with some harsh truths about herself, which are very hard for her to stomach.

There is a theme of prejudice running through the play. I felt then and still feel that racial prejudice does not stand alone. It is masking something else, like ignorance or fear or bitterness or envy or powerlessness or misplaced patriotism. And it's evil. In the beginning Rosinella's prejudice against the Scots, seen first of all in her banter with Franco, is mildly amusing. However, it makes her say and do some terrible things, the worst and most consequential of which is her dismissal of Bridget when she comes looking for news of Franco. When I was writing the play, I felt I was building to the moment when she is confronted with her own prejudice. In the big scene with Massimo he was going to accuse her directly of being prejudiced, but when I came to write it I realised there was no need for him to say it. The audience should have seen it for themselves by now. What he does accuse her of is total selfishness, of being so consumed with her own longing for children that she was indifferent to his. I think it is worth asking: *What is Rosinella's prejudice really? What is it masking?*

Now what about Hughie? Wee Hughie? Only Hughie? His relationship with Lucia is central to the play and becomes crucial to Rosinella, as she comes to see him as a threat to her hold over Lucia. In many ways his relationship with Lucia mirrors Massimo's with Rosinella, insofar as he gives in to her at every turn. A question I asked myself when I was writing it was: *Why does he love her?* Why would this good, decent little boy love a bossy little madam like Lucia? The scene in the ginger store just after Hughie's dad dies was written to answer this question. She gives him something that no-one else does and which he desperately needs. She makes him cry for his dad. Everyone else is telling him not to cry, to be a big brave boy and nobody is letting him grieve. Even though Lucia admits that she can turn on the tears to get what she wants, when they go off crying together, arms around each other, it is my hope that, in the audience's mind, these two belong together.

When I am struggling with a scene, or writing something and it isn't working, I try to pull back and remind myself of this very simple truth about drama. Drama lies in what is going on between people at an emotional level. I drum this into my students. In *Tally's Blood*, the themes are important, the setting is important and the war is important, but the drama lies in what is happening between the characters in the scenes. Rosinella telling Bridget that Italian boys play around with Scottish girls but marry Italians is not meant as a social commentary or comparison of cultures. It is deeply offensive and devastates Bridget. In this scene Rosinella is nasty, unfeeling and cruel. She is also hurting and frightened herself. It is what is going on *emotionally* between these two women that creates the drama. It is worth comparing the emotions of this scene with the final scene between Rosinella and Bridget, in which Bridget tells Rosinella about the abortion.

It might be of interest to note that in the very first production of the play, the director cut Massimo's monologue about the *Arandora Star*. He felt the play was too long and also that, stylistically, it stuck out like a sore thumb. I take his point about the style, but I reinstated the speech later and for subsequent productions it has always been there. It does break from the style of the play, which is otherwise completely naturalistic, but it means so much to me personally that I want to keep it. I feel that this moment in the play lights a candle to the victims of the *Arandora Star*. It is strongly based on events which happened to my father when he was arrested and interned during the war. He pleaded to be allowed onto that ship because all his friends were going on it but he was forced back. The scene does give a lot of information but does not really move the story on. We really don't *have* to know exactly what happened to Massimo. However, perhaps it helps to inform the character of Massimo, who has no bitterness about his experiences compared to Rosinella, for whom the war reinforces all her prejudices.

I am very gratified that you are studying *Tally's Blood*. I hope it speaks to you, a whole new generation. For although the means of communication have changed since 1990, people have remained the same. We're still trying to make sense of the world. We still want things we can't have. We still try our best and make mistakes, infuriate, misunderstand, judge, mistreat, disappoint and, all too often, hurt each other. We love and laugh and hope and fear and dance and play and so much more. This is the stuff of life. This is what drama is about. I hope you find the stuff of life in *Tally's Blood*.

Ann Marie Di Mambro

October 2013

Publisher's Note: The image on the front of this book is from the original poster used to promote the Traverse Theatre's production of *Tally's Blood* in 1990. The main picture was taken in approximately 1944 and shows The Cosy Corner Café in Hamilton that belonged to the author's grandparents. Her grandmother, Rosaria, and her uncle, Carmino Cocozza, are the two people on either side of the door, and the rest of the images are from the author's private collection of photographs and letters.

List of characters

In order of appearance

Rosinella Pedreschi

Massimo Pedreschi, a shopkeeper, Rosinella's husband

Lucia Ianelli, niece of Rosinella and Massimo

Luigi Ianelli, Lucia's father and Rosinella's brother-in-law

Franco Pedreschi, Massimo's younger brother

Hughie Devlin

Bridget Devlin, Hughie's eldest sister

Tally's Blood
Act One

Italian pronunciation guide

Names

Lucia	loo-<u>chee</u>-a
Luigi	loo-<u>eej</u>-ay
Pedreschi	paid-<u>rays</u>-key
Ianelli	yan-<u>ell</u>-ee

Act One

Scene One	*dorme* [she's sleeping]		<u>dor</u>-may
	sempre [still]		<u>same</u>-pray
Scene Two	*ciao* [hello]	<u>cha</u>-ow	
	Song:	jo-van-<u>ates</u>-a	
		preem-a-<u>vair</u>-a dee bell-<u>ates</u>-a	
		day-la <u>vee</u>-ta, nay-la-<u>spray</u>-tsa	
		eel too-oh <u>can</u>-toe squeel ay <u>va</u>	
	Song:	<u>par</u>-la-my da-<u>more</u>-ay, mar-<u>you</u>	
Scene Four	*ti piace*	tee pee-<u>ach</u>-ee	
	mi	mee	
	la scuola	la <u>skoo</u>-ol-a	
	parla	<u>par</u>-la	
	inglese	ing-<u>glaze</u>-ay	
	italiano	ee-<u>tal</u>-ee-<u>an</u>-o	
Scene Thirteen	*marito mio*		ma-<u>reet</u>-oh <u>mee</u>-oh
	e morto [he's dead]		eh <u>mor</u>-toe

Scene One

Year: 1936: Italy/Night

'Santa Lucia' playing softly: sound of mourning bell in background.

Lights up on Rosinella and Luigi.

*Rosinella ready for a journey. Luigi with black armband round
his upper arm. With great care he is handing a blanket with a
sleeping child over to Rosinella. They speak in whispers.*

ROSINELLA: Dorme?

LUIGI: Sì. Dorme sempre.

ROSINELLA: (*Fingers to her lips*) Sshh ...

*Luigi takes a last look inside the blanket, then embraces Rosinella,
kissing her on both cheeks. He strokes the blanket and abruptly
turns away, unable to deal with the pain. He holds his hand out
behind him to prevent further contact.*

*Rosinella is aware of Massimo in background, standing with suitcase.
He picks it up and comes to Rosinella, puts an arm protectively
round her shoulder and leads her away.*

Scene Two

Year: 1939: Pedreschi's back shop

Lucia (age five) preening in brand new party frock and shoes: doing a twirl.

Rosinella and Massimo up to her, fussing over her with delight: she loves it.

MASSIMO: Oh, who's that lovely wee girl?

ROSINELLA: Turn round, hen.

MASSIMO: Isn't she lovely?

ROSINELLA: And do you see the lovely wee shoes she's got?

Lucia shows them off.

MASSIMO: Oh, would you look at those. You know what they call them, don't you? Those are 'kissing shoes'.

She holds up her feet one at a time and he kisses her shoes: she giggles.

ROSINELLA: She's a lucky wee girl. Your Uncle Massimo had to make a lot of ice cream to get you that nice dress. (*Rosinella takes ribbons out of a bag and holds them up to the dress.*) And look, we got the wee ribbons to match. (*To Massimo*) The shop been busy?

MASSIMO: (*Shrugs*) So so.

ROSINELLA: And she got a new schoolbag for starting the school. Go get it, Lucia.

Lucia goes to get her bag.

Massimo pulls Rosinella aside, whispers.

MASSIMO: Listen, Rosie, I thought you went to Glasgow to buy yourself a new coat.

ROSINELLA: Oh, but see when I saw that wee dress I just had to get her it. My heart's breaking for that wee lassie these days.

MASSIMO: She's just a wean. She'll no understand.

ROSINELLA: But she's lovely in it, isn't she?

MASSIMO: Don't get me wrong. I don't grudge the wean a frock. God forbid. It's just you I'm worried about. Last year when I gave you money for a coat you bought jumpers to send to Italy.

ROSINELLA: So?

Massimo smiles with great affection, squeezes her cheek between his thumb and forefinger.

MASSIMO: So what have I to do with you, you daft wee besom, you?

Lucia comes back carrying her schoolbag: Massimo takes it from her.

MASSIMO: Oh, is this what I got? Let me see. Oh, that's great, so it is. Just what I was needing for bringing home the tatties. Oh here, it's awfy wee. You better just take it, Lucia.

He pretends to put it on: Lucia giggles.

LUCIA: Uncle Massimo, you're awful silly.

ROSINELLA: Now away you go, Lucia, and take off your lovely dress.

LUCIA: (*Mood changing/petulant*) I want to keep it on.

ROSINELLA: (*Coaxing*) You need to take it off, love.

LUCIA: No.

MASSIMO: Keep it nice for something special.

LUCIA: No.

ROSINELLA: If you take it off now I'll let you wear it to mass this Sunday.

LUCIA: I want to keep it on.

ROSINELLA: Come on, hen.

LUCIA: I'm keeping it on, I says.

MASSIMO: You better no let her away with that.

ROSINELLA: Come on, darling, we'll get you changed.

LUCIA: (*Starting to shout*) No, no, no.

ROSINELLA: (*Voice raised but pleading*) Now Lucia!

Massimo glances over shoulder in direction of front shop.

LUCIA: I don't want to. I don't want to.

MASSIMO: Sshh! You two. I've got customers out there. (*To Lucia*) Do what your Auntie Rosinella tells you, darling, there's a good girl.

Rosinella takes Lucia's arm to lead her away.

ROSINELLA: Come on, Lucia.

Lucia starts to scream and pull back.

LUCIA: No, no, no, leave me alone, I want to keep it on. I want to keep it on. No – no – no –

Rosinella and Massimo look helplessly at each other. Massimo also keeps glancing in direction of shop, anxious to get back.

ROSINELLA: (*Appealing*) Massimo.

MASSIMO: Maybe you're being too hard on her.

ROSINELLA: Me?

MASSIMO: Why no let her keep it on for a wee while, eh?

ROSINELLA: Just a wee while, then, OK.

Lucia controls her sobs (she's won).

LUCIA: OK.

MASSIMO: Just this once.

LUCIA: OK.

ROSINELLA: Seeing it's new.

MASSIMO: Now don't be getting it dirty, mind.

ROSINELLA: There's a good girl.

MASSIMO: Here. Come here. You're forgetting your Uncle Massimo's got a shop to run, eh?

He pulls her to him, hugs her, takes out his hanky: wipes her eyes, wipes her nose.

Blow! Ach, what use is that? I said 'blow' – like this.

He gives an almighty blow in the hanky: she giggles: he holds hanky for her to blow her nose.

That's better.

Now – one here. And one here.

He points to his cheeks one after the other and she kisses them.

Who's my best girl?

Rosinella looking on, adoring.

FRANCO: (*Voice from offstage: singing*) Parlami d'amore, Mariù …

LUCIA: Uncle Franco.

She jumps up with excitement and runs to meet him coming in. He comes in from front shop: she jumps into his arms and he swings her around and she laughs, delighted. He puts her down and holds her back to look at her.

Massimo goes out to the front shop.

FRANCO: Oh, who's a lovely girl the day?

ROSINELLA: You like her new dress, Uncle Franco?

FRANCO: (*To Lucia*) Did you miss me, then, eh? Wait to you see this, wait to you see this.

Takes a coin from his pocket, tosses it, puts both hands behind his back, holds both out, fists clenched.

LUCIA: That one.

She opens his fist. It's empty.

He laughs, opens his other fist and gives her the coin.

LUCIA: Look what Uncle Franco gave me.

FRANCO: There's some queue out there. Will I give Massimo a hand to shift it?

ROSINELLA: He can manage on his own for a wee while. I want a word with you, Franco.

She looks round, sees Lucia, ears cocked.

ROSINELLA: Away you go into the shop, Lucia, pick a wee
sweetie.

Lucia goes reluctantly, knowing she's missing something.

ROSINELLA: (*For Lucia's benefit*) We're doing awfy well with the
hot peas just now.

Rosinella glad to get Franco on his own.

ROSINELLA: Tell me about Luigi.

FRANCO: I've told you.

ROSINELLA: Tell me again.

Franco goes to speak: but doesn't get the chance.

ROSINELLA: (*Indignant*) Never took him long, did it? It's no
two years past since my sister died. Crying his heart out, so
he was, had everybody crying. And look at him now, eh?

FRANCO: So he got married again. You can hardly blame
him for that.

ROSINELLA: Oh, there'll be something in it for him, likely.
Takes everything that's going. Don't know what he
thinks he's playing at. Starting a new family, he cannie
even take care of the one he's got.

FRANCO: Good luck to him.

ROSINELLA: And what am I supposed to tell her, eh?
(*Pointing in direction of Lucia*) Your daddy's got a new wife,
a new baby, he's forgotten all about you?

FRANCO: Now you know that's no fair.

ROSINELLA: Well, what's it look like to you?

FRANCO: See you! Once you make up your mind about something ...

ROSINELLA: (*Interrupting/at full flow*) Couldn't even tell us himself, could he? If you hadn't went off to Italy we'd probably still no know. How often did you see him? Did he come to see you? Did you go to see him? Did he talk about Lucia? Did he ask about his lassie? I have to know. I want to know everything.

Franco has been trying to get a word in.

FRANCO: Just suppose I told you he's miserable without her, he cannie wait to get her back. For good!

Rosinella clutches her heart.

ROSINELLA: He is not?

FRANCO: He might be.

ROSINELLA: He cannie be.

FRANCO: But what if he was?

ROSINELLA: Ach – he knows his lassie's better off here. Anyway he's got enough on his hands right now with his new baby boy. (*Franco sniggers*) What you laughing at, you?

FRANCO: You.

ROSINELLA: (*Mock annoyance*) I'll fix you.

Massimo pops head in from front shop: shouts.

MASSIMO: Two teas and two hot oranges.

Rosinella starts to make it.

ROSINELLA: How's your daddy?

FRANCO: Crabbit as ever.

ROSINELLA: Enjoyed his holiday?

FRANCO: Alright, I suppose. (*A beat*) Says to tell you to go
    up tonight and cut his toenails.

ROSINELLA: (*Scoffs*) I've to laugh at him. Isn't talking to us,
    mind you, but still wants me to run after him.

FRANCO: What did our Massimo have to open up his own
    shop for, anyway?

ROSINELLA: Oh Franco, now don't you start. We get
    enough of that from your daddy.

FRANCO: No! It's no that I blame him. It's just that, since
    he left, it's worse for me now. Stuck in that shop with
    that moaning old git and I know I'm no going to stick it
    much longer.

ROSINELLA: What else can you do?

FRANCO: I can get out.

ROSINELLA: The pits or the steelworks – that's all there is round here.

FRANCO: There must be something else. There must be. Look at me. I'm young – I cannie be expected to spend my whole life working from morning to night in a wee pokey shop. Apart from anything else, so long as I'm there he's got a hold over me.

Massimo in.

MASSIMO: (*To Rosinella*) You'll never guess who's dead?

ROSINELLA: (*Interested*) Who?

MASSIMO: You'll never guess.

ROSINELLA: Don't tell me.

MASSIMO: You mind a Sanny?

ROSINELLA: Sanny?

MASSIMO: You mind a Sanny? Big Sanny?

ROSINELLA: Big Sanny? From the Auld Toon?

MASSIMO: Aye.

ROSINELLA: Big face? Dark hair?

MASSIMO: Aye.

ROSINELLA: Worked with the bins?

MASSIMO: Did he?

ROSINELLA: Aye. Never married.

MASSIMO: Aye. (*A beat*) Naw. I'll tell you who you're thinking of. You're thinking of Wee Sanny.

ROSINELLA: Wee Sanny?

MASSIMO: Wee Sanny Mulligan. I'm talking about Big Sanny. Big Sanny Kerrigan.

ROSINELLA: Ah! That Sanny? Sanny Kerrigan? You mean he's deid?

MASSIMO: Who says he was dead?

ROSINELLA: You did.

MASSIMO: No him. His next-door neighbour. Dropped dead at the bookie's. His wife had his dinner on too. (*A beat. Turns to Franco*) Where are you off to the night, Frankie-boy?

FRANCO: That reminds me, Rosinella. I told ma faither I was going to the Casa to play cards with Massimo. Mind and back me up when you see him.

ROSINELLA: How? Where are you going?

MASSIMO: These ready?

Picks up tray and goes.

FRANCO: I've got a date on.

ROSINELLA: (*Disapproving*) Who with?

Franco smiles, touches his nose.

ROSINELLA: A Scotch girl?

Franco winks.

ROSINELLA: I'm right, amn't I?

FRANCO: Could be.

ROSINELLA: You better watch these lassies. (*Franco scoffs*) Who is it anyway? Anybody I know?

FRANCO: (*Face lights up talking about her*) This is not 'anybody'. It's Bridget Devlin. You know her?

ROSINELLA: (*Disapproving*) From the Auld Toon? Adam Devlin's lassie?

FRANCO: What if she is?

ROSINELLA: No harm to the lassie, Franco, but look at that family. Must be six or seven weans.

FRANCO: Eight.

ROSINELLA: (*Shocked*) Eight weans! She keeps having them and she cannie even look after them right. And look at me! It's no fair, is it. Twelve years I've been married – and nothing. Me an Italian as well.

FRANCO: They're a great family, Rosinella. Really close.

ROSINELLA: You never met anybody in Italy?

FRANCO: I wasn't looking.

ROSINELLA: I says to Massimo, I wouldn't be surprised if
you come back engaged.

FRANCO: I told you, Rosinella, I've got someone.

ROSINELLA: You're surely no keen on this Scotch girl?

FRANCO: What if I am?

ROSINELLA: Then she must be giving you something you
can't get from an Italian girl. I'm telling you, you better
watch yourself.

FRANCO: You know nothing about Bridget.

ROSINELLA: Now you listen good to me, son. These Scotch
girls, they're all the same. They just go out with you for
one thing. Because your faither's got a shop and they
think you've got money.

FRANCO: (*Indignant*) Thanks very much.

ROSINELLA: Alright. Alright. And because you're tall …

FRANCO: Good looking …

ROSINELLA: You're good fun to be with …

FRANCO: … a good kisser, a good dancer …

ROSINELLA: Aye, but that's because you're Italian.

FRANCO: Oh, they like that alright. All I have to do is say
     'Ciao Bella' and they're all over me.

Lucia in from front shop.

     Ciao Bella.

She jumps on his back for a piggyback.

     See what I mean?

ROSINELLA: Listen – these girls. (*Lowers voice so Lucia won't
     hear*) Don't think I don't understand. You're no different
     from all the other Italian men. You're young, you've got
     the warm blood. But it's one thing to play around with
     them, so long as you marry your own kind. You watch
     none of them catches you. That's the kind of thing they
     do here.

FRANCO: What?

ROSINELLA: They see a man they want and – you know –
     they know how to make sure they get him.

FRANCO: (*Cheeky*) That's good coming from you, Rosie,
     seeing as how you got yours.

ROSINELLA: (*Shocked*) Franco Pedreschi!

FRANCO: I didn't mean anything.

ROSINELLA: In front of the wean too.

Massimo in.

ROSINELLA: Talk to him, Massimo.

MASSIMO: Hello, Franco.

Rosinella cuffs Massimo.

ROSINELLA: And you're no better.

*Franco starts to march with Lucia on his back, singing: after the
first couple of words Massimo joins in, conducting with his
finger. Rosinella pretends to despair, but is loving every minute.
Massimo takes her hands and dances her round, pulling her into
the song.*

FRANCO AND MASSIMO: Giovinezza, giovinezza,
    Primavera di bellezza,
    Della vita, nell'asprezza
    Il tuo canto squilla e va ...

    Giovinezza, giovinezza ...

Scene Three

Same evening: Street

Hughie, scruffy-looking, short trousers, dribbling his football.

Franco enters from opposite side of stage.

FRANCO: Here, Hughie.

Hughie kicks it to him, they kick it around a bit, Franco picks up ball and takes it to him and ruffles his hair.

FRANCO: How you doing, Hughie son?

HUGHIE: Alright.

FRANCO: You starting the school soon?

HUGHIE: Worse luck.

Franco takes coin from his pocket: Hughie's eyes light up, don't leave the coin.

FRANCO: See your big sister –

HUGHIE: What one?

FRANCO: Bridget. Who else?

HUGHIE: What about her?

FRANCO: Do you ever hear her talking about me?

HUGHIE: Who to?

Franco tosses coin, catches it, puts both hands behind his back.

FRANCO: To anyone. Have you ever heard her saying
    anything about me?

HUGHIE: Like what?

Franco brings his clenched fists out and holds them in front of Hughie.

FRANCO: Oh, I don't know – maybe something like she likes
    me, or she thinks I'm nice. What hand is it in?

HUGHIE: No really. That one.

Franco opens his hand.

FRANCO: Wrong.

HUGHIE: Anyway, why don't you ask her yourself? She's
    standing over there.

*Franco looks over his shoulder: Bridget is standing: he opens his other
    fist and gives Hughie the coin.*

FRANCO: Here y'are, son.

*Franco pats him on head and goes over to Bridget who is looking the other
    way: he pauses, runs fingers through his hair, gets his pose ready.*

FRANCO: Ciao Bella!

BRIDGET: (*Melting*) Oh Franco, hello.

FRANCO: Buona sera.

BRIDGET: I like your tan.

FRANCO: It's all over my body – except for my –

BRIDGET: (*Interrupting*) Did you miss me?

FRANCO: Did I miss you? Did I miss you?

BRIDGET: What about all those lovely girls in Italy?

FRANCO: Never clapped eyes on them.

Bridget scoffs.

FRANCO: Honest to God. They're no allowed past the
    doorstep. And see if you fancy someone over there
    you've to go to the house and sit with the whole
    family.

BRIDGET: And how would you know?

FRANCO: Rosinella told me. Look, I brought you a present.

BRIDGET: Oh, Franco.

FRANCO: It's a wee corneet.

BRIDGET: A what?

FRANCO: An Italian good luck charm. You can wear it on a
    chain.

BRIDGET: I don't have a chain.

FRANCO: Or a bracelet.

BRIDGET: I haven't got a bracelet either.

FRANCO: You could even put it on a watch.

Bridget laughs.

FRANCO: Don't tell me – you don't have a watch.

BRIDGET: It doesn't matter. I still love it.

FRANCO: I'm sorry it's so wee. But it's real gold.

BRIDGET: Thank you. (*She kisses him*)

FRANCO: In Italy, if you like someone, you buy them gold.

BRIDGET: Is that right?

FRANCO: So, what have you been up to while I was away?

BRIDGET: Never been out the door. (*Sees Franco's look of disbelief*) Honest to God. And my da's driving us mad. Does nothing but talk about war. Him and his cronies. 'There's going to be a war. There's going to be a war. We were in the last war. We know the signs.' I'm glad just to get out.

FRANCO: (*Indignant*) Just – to get out?

BRIDGET: No. To see you.

FRANCO: Good. Let's go.

He offers his arm and she snuggles in.

FRANCO: (*Sings*) Parlami d'amore ... Bridget.

They go off.

Scene Four

Back of shop: A few weeks later

Rosinella and Massimo: mid-discussion.

MASSIMO: You're sure that's what she said?

ROSINELLA: Sure as God's my judge standing here. Says
we've to stop speaking Italian in the house. What do you
make of that, eh?

Franco in.

ROSINELLA: Ciao, Franco. She says Lucia won't speak the right
English in the school. Then, she says, if she doesn't talk
she'll no can get on with her reading. (*To Franco*) You want
a wee cup of coffee? So we've no to talk Italian in the house.

FRANCO: But you two talk English most of the time.

ROSINELLA: I told her that. I says Lucia speaks the good
English. But she says she's collapsed back into Italian.

MASSIMO: Come to think of it, Lucia has been speaking
Italian these days. Where is she?

ROSINELLA: Upstairs.

MASSIMO: Get her down.

ROSINELLA: (*Shouts at top of her voice*) Lucia!

Massimo rubs his ear.

MASSIMO: I could've done that.

Lucia, huffy, pokes head downstairs.

LUCIA: Cos' è?

MASSIMO: Come here, hen.

Lucia comes down: Massimo lifts her up and kneels her on the table: they crowd round her.

FRANCO: You like the school hen?

LUCIA: Non lo so.

ROSINELLA: She does like it. Sure you do, hen?

LUCIA: Non mi piace la scuola.

MASSIMO: Yes, you do.

ROSINELLA: Speak English, Lucia.

MASSIMO: You have to speak English.

LUCIA: Non mi piace l'inglese.

ROSINELLA: Say that in English.

Their speech gathers momentum and volume: Lucia pulls more and more into herself.

FRANCO: Your teacher says you've to speak English.

MASSIMO: Parla inglese. Non italiano.

ROSINELLA: (*Annoyed/to Massimo*) Ma, tu parla inglese!

FRANCO: All the other wee boys and girls speak English.

ROSINELLA: You don't want them laughing at you, do you?

FRANCO: You want to do well at school, don't you?

ROSINELLA: Speak English, Lucia.

MASSIMO: Parla inglese.

ROSINELLA: Let me hear you say something.

FRANCO: You need to speak English at the school.

ROSINELLA: You speak good English, don't you, Lucia?

MASSIMO: Speak English.

ROSINELLA: Parla inglese.

FRANCO: Say something.

ROSINELLA: Something in English.

MASSIMO: There's a good girl.

ROSINELLA: Speak English.

MASSIMO: Parla inglese.

FRANCO: Say something.

*They are now like vultures round her, repeating 'Speak English',
    'Parla inglese', 'Say something', until Lucia breaks.*

LUCIA: (*Screams*) Fuck off!

Stunned silence.

MASSIMO: You bloody bitch!

He slaps Lucia.

*Typical Italian volatile fight erupts (possibly some in Italian) with
    much pointing of fingers and nose-to-nose contact: Lucia howling
    in time to it.*

Rosinella slaps Massimo.

ROSINELLA: Don't you dare hit that wean.

MASSIMO: And don't you hit me.

ROSINELLA: Don't you ever hit that wean.

FRANCO: Now don't you two start.

ROSINELLA: And don't you call her a 'bloody bitch'.

FRANCO: Will you calm down, the pair of you?

MASSIMO: The wee bugger swore.

ROSINELLA: My sister would turn in her grave.

FRANCO: Rosinella!

MASSIMO: You cannie let a wean swear. She's got to learn.

FRANCO: Massimo!

ROSINELLA: Turn in her grave with her legs up.

FRANCO: Are you going to pack it in? You're upsetting the wean.

ROSINELLA: What's it to do with you?

FRANCO: I'm only trying to help.

ROSINELLA: I'll deal with it. Me!

MASSIMO: He's just trying to help.

ROSINELLA: I'll deal with it. OK?

By this point Lucia's howls are deafening.

FRANCO, MASSIMO AND ROSINELLA: (*To Lucia*) Shut up!

Silence: The three adults look guiltily from one to the other: Lucia starts to sob gently: they talk softly, cajoling.

ROSINELLA: There there, darling, it's alright.

FRANCO: It's alright now, Lucia.

MASSIMO: Don't cry, now, there's a good girl. You know I hate to see you cry.

FRANCO: It's all finished now.

MASSIMO: Come to your Uncle Massimo. Come on, we'll pick a wee sweetie. Come on. Hup – two – three. There you go.

He takes her on his back: Rosinella and Franco watch them go.

ROSINELLA: (*Shrugs*) She's only a wean.

FRANCO: What'll happen if there's a war, Rosie? Will you send her back?

ROSINELLA: What are you talking about?

FRANCO: I mean, if we go into war, she might be better off over there, out the road of it.

ROSINELLA: What's it got to do with us? We just live here. It's no even our country.

FRANCO: I'm just saying –

ROSINELLA: (*Cutting him off*) Then don't.

FRANCO: (*Gently*) She's not your lassie, Rosinella. You're getting to love her too much. That's all I'm saying.

He squeezes her arm and goes out through the front shop.

Scene Five

Same day: Street outside Pedreschi's

*Hughie in, gets his marbles out of his pocket and sets up and starts
   to play: Massimo sweeping out his shop, spots him, comes and
   stands beside him. Hughie, nose to the ground to fire his marble.
   It hits off Massimo's boot. Hughie stares at the boot then raises
   his eyes slowly, up Massimo's body, to his face.*

MASSIMO: Sorry if I wasted your plunk, son.

*Hughie picks up the marble: Massimo crouches down beside him:
   holds out his hand: Hughie gives him it.*

MASSIMO: Let me see. What do you call this one?

HUGHIE: My 'whitey'.

MASSIMO: Can I have a go?

HUGHIE: Aye.

Massimo starts to play with the marbles.

MASSIMO: You're Adam Devlin's boy, am I right?

HUGHIE: Aye.

MASSIMO: Knew it soon as I looked at you. You're his double.
   A good man, your faither. Still working at the pits?

HUGHIE: Aye.

MASSIMO: Don't say much, do you?

HUGHIE: Aye. I mean, no.

MASSIMO: Do you go to the school?

HUGHIE: Aye.

MASSIMO: Saint Mary's.

HUGHIE: Aye.

MASSIMO: And would you know a wee lassie called Lucia Ianelli? She goes to your school as well.

HUGHIE: Aye. (*Massimo just about exasperated with the 'ayes'*) She's in my class.

MASSIMO: Listen son, would you like to do a wee job for me?

HUGHIE: Aye, what?

MASSIMO: I'm needing somebody to tidy up the ginger store. I'll pay you, and you can help yourself to a wee bottle of ginger.

HUGHIE: Alright.

Enthusiastic: he rushes off: Massimo grabs him back.

MASSIMO: Hang on. You don't know where it is yet.

HUGHIE: Oh aye, right.

MASSIMO: I'll show you. Oh, and if you see Lucia I want you to talk to her – in English.

HUGHIE: (*Confused*) What? You mean posh?

MASSIMO: (*Amused /exasperated*) No son, just talk.

Hughie gathers up the marbles and Massimo ruffles his hair and points in direction of ginger store: Hughie goes: Massimo starts to sweep again.

Franco in.

FRANCO: She's calmed down now.

MASSIMO: She's a wee soul. Come here, Franco. What are you thinking about all this talk? Is there going to be a war or what?

FRANCO: If it comes to it, then there could be. We cannie let that wee German bastard throw his weight around.

MASSIMO: I hope and pray it's just talk. Nobody really wants a war.

FRANCO: I know a lot of people who do.

MASSIMO: Like who, for instance?

FRANCO: A lot of the young guys that come into the shop. To hear them talk you'd think they cannie wait.

MASSIMO: It's just talk, son. Don't you listen to them.

FRANCO: Listen Massie, I better go. I'm going out the night. Oh and by the way, I told ma faither ...

MASSIMO: ... you were playing cards with me. Right, right. I get the picture.

Franco goes: Massimo carries on sweeping.

Pick up on ginger store: Hughie deeply engrossed in tidying the crates. Stops and surveys it with satisfaction. Takes a bottle of ginger and drinks from it. Enter Lucia, indignant when she sees him. She goes right up to him, eyeing him up and down suspiciously: Hughie keeps drinking from the bottle.

LUCIA: (*Increasingly self-righteous*) Hughie Devlin! What are you doing here? ... Who says you could come in here? ... This is my Uncle Massimo's ginger store ... This is my Uncle Massimo's whole shop, so it is ... Everything in here is my Uncle Massimo's ... Did you ask for that ginger? ... That's my Uncle Massimo's ginger ... I'm going to tell my Uncle Massimo on you ... I'm telling him you took his ginger ... You better not take any more of that ginger ...

Hughie takes the bottle from his mouth and involuntarily lets out an almighty belch: she is horrified, punches him on the upper arm.

LUCIA: You stop that, you!

Hughie hands her the bottle.

HUGHIE: Want a slug?

Lucia turns away in disgust.

LUCIA: No thank you.

HUGHIE: You can if you want. It's my ginger.

Lucia scoffs.

HUGHIE: Honest. It is. Mr Pedreschi says I'd to help myself.

LUCIA: How come?

HUGHIE: (*Chuffed*) Because I work here, that's how come.

LUCIA: You do not.

HUGHIE: I do so. (*A beat*) Want a slug?

*Lucia eyes the bottle then slowly takes it: she makes a great show of
wiping the top of it with the palm of her hand. Looks Hughie
in the eye then does it again, very hard. Then she pulls the
sleeve of her jumper down over her hand and rubs the bottle
feverishly with it before deigning to put it to her lips. She
takes a dainty little sip. Hughie watches carefully. She takes
another little sip. Finally she tilts her head back and takes
huge gulps, thoroughly enjoying it. Hughie is right up to her,
examining the bottle and her progress with its contents with
some concern.*

HUGHIE: If you get my chewing gum in your mouth will you
spit it back into the bottle?

*With a horrified scream, Lucia stops, spits out the liquid from her
mouth, showering Hughie.*

*Bring up romantic/waltzy music: Franco and Bridget waltz in,
Hughie and Lucia creep behind ginger boxes (unseen by
audience if possible).*

*Fade down the music, Franco carries on humming it: Franco is a good
     dancer, Bridget is not, she stands on his toes, they stop.
     She laughs, embarrassed.*

BRIDGET: Sorry, Franco, I done it again.

FRANCO: It's alright, it's not the same foot.

BRIDGET: I told you I cannie dance. My da'll no let us go to
     the dancing.

FRANCO: Green's Playhouse, Thursday nights. That's how I
     learnt.

BRIDGET: Says lassies just cheapen themselves. Getting all
     done up to stand in a line to wait for some man to dance
     with them. He says half the time you don't even know
     who you're dancing with.

FRANCO: He'd let you come with me, surely?

BRIDGET: Maybe – but I still cannie dance.

Franco puts his arms round her again.

FRANCO: Who needs to dance? It's just nice to get my arms
     round you.

They kiss: she pulls away, looks round.

FRANCO: It's OK. Nobody will come in. Come on. Sit down.

*He sits with his back to the crates, pats the ground beside him: she sits:
     he puts his arm round her: they kiss again: a giggle from behind
     the stack of crates. Bridget sits up.*

BRIDGET: What was that?

FRANCO: Relax, Bridget. You're a bag of nerves.

They kiss again. Hughie's head appears behind the ginger crates: the kissing gets more passionate: Hughie's mouth opens wide in amazement: Bridget breaks free, Hughie's head disappears.

BRIDGET: We better stop, Franco. We could get carried away.

FRANCO: I won't go all the way, I promise.

They kiss again. Hughie's head appears behind the crates again: Bridget breaks free and sits up: Hughie's head disappears.

BRIDGET: I'm sorry. (*A beat*) Can we not just ... talk?

Franco sighs, puts his hands behind his head, leans back.

BRIDGET: Have you told your da about me yet?

FRANCO: There's no need.

BRIDGET: (*Indignant*) And what am I supposed to make of that?

FRANCO: See women! I didn't mean anything, alright! All I'm saying is I'm biding my time till I get out that shop. Then it doesn't matter anymore what he thinks. Alright?

BRIDGET: Listen, Franco, I don't want you leaving your da's shop because of me.

FRANCO: What's that supposed to mean?

BRIDGET: I don't want to be the cause of any bust-up between you and your da. You'd only blame me for it later.

FRANCO: Come here, you. (*He kisses her*) I've worked in that shop for as long as I can remember, and for as long as I can remember I've thought about getting out. Coming in from school, straight behind the counter. Saturdays, Sundays, the lot. I might've done something different but what chance had I?

BRIDGET: Poor wee love. (*She makes an affectionate clucking noise and kisses him gently*) I've heard it all before, Franco. 'I could have been a brain surgeon but I was tied to ma faither's shop.' You'll never get out.

FRANCO: I will.

BRIDGET: You're just like the rest of the men round here. All you can do is talk.

FRANCO: (*Sings*) Parlami d'amore, Mariù.

BRIDGET: Alright – and sing. (*A beat*) Who's Mariù? Some wee girl you met in Italy?

FRANCO: That's just the song.

BRIDGET: Sing me the rest of it.

FRANCO: I can't.

BRIDGET: Why not?

FRANCO: I only know the one line.

BRIDGET: Typical! Sing me something else, then.

FRANCO: Like what?

BRIDGET: (*Settling back to enjoy it*) Something Italian. I love to hear Italian, so I do.

FRANCO: (*Sings*) 'Giovinezza, giovinezza, primavera di bellezza.' I learnt that in Italy. Everyone was singing it. On the radio. In the streets. 'Giovinezza, giovinezza' – that means young people, young people, 'Primavera di bellezza' – the spring time of ... beautiful things.

BRIDGET: That's beautiful.

FRANCO: (*Sings*) Giovinezza, giovinezza
Primavera di bellezza ...

He slows down, aware of a wee voice behind the ginger boxes, singing along with him.

It is Lucia: she carries on alone.

LUCIA: (*Voice from offstage: quietly*) Della vita, nell'asprezza
Il tuo canto squilla e va.

Franco jumps up and looks behind the ginger boxes: Bridget scrambles to her feet.

BRIDGET: If you tell our da about this, Hughie Devlin, I'll ...
    I'll ...

FRANCO: (*Bellows*) Get your arses out of there, the pair of
    you, before I murder you ... Go on ... Scram!

The kids scarper.

Scene Six

A week later

Scene intercut between Massimo and Rosinella in back shop and Hughie and Lucia in ginger store.

Lights up on Rosinella and Massimo.

MASSIMO: You'll never guess who's dead?

Pick up on Hughie and Lucia.

Hughie is standing facing the crates of ginger, back to Lucia, head bowed: Lucia standing near him, horror struck.

LUCIA: Hughie? You're in here?

Pick up on Rosinella: she is blessing herself.

MASSIMO: They say it happened quick. He wouldn't have felt anything. A wee build up of gas down the pit and Adam Devlin got the worst of it. A good man too.

ROSINELLA: His poor wife.

MASSIMO: Poor wee Hughie.

Pick up on Lucia and Hughie again: as before, Lucia finding it difficult to cope with Hughie's silence.

LUCIA: (*Almost pleading*) You going to cry?

Hughie shakes his head.

LUCIA: Are you not? Are you not going to cry?

Hughie shakes his head.

LUCIA: How come you're not going to cry?

HUGHIE: I'm no supposed to cry.

LUCIA: Who says?

HUGHIE: Everybody. I've to be the big brave man. I've to be strong for my mammy. I'm not going to cry. I cannie cry.

LUCIA: I'm great at crying, so I am. I can cry whenever I like.

Hughie silent.

LUCIA: If I want something I'm not supposed to get, I just ... cry.

Hughie silent.

LUCIA: My Auntie Rosinella says your daddy's in heaven.

Hughie silent.

LUCIA: Did they make you see your daddy dead?

Hughie silent.

LUCIA: I remember the night my mammy went to heaven. It was great. I was just wee and they kept passing me round one to the other and kissing me and crying. And I was crying all the time. Then they took me in to see my mammy dead. They said, look at your mammy, she's only sleeping, she's beautiful. Then they lifted me up and said kiss your mammy. And I did. But she was cold. Really cold. Poor mammy.

HUGHIE: She'll be alright now.

LUCIA: How?

HUGHIE: She will. She'll be alright. She's got my daddy to look after her.

LUCIA: Look at your shoes, Hughie Devlin. Where have you been?

HUGHIE: Nowhere.

LUCIA: You've been down at the river. You're not allowed down there.

HUGHIE: I have not.

LUCIA: You have so.

HUGHIE: I have not.

LUCIA: Yes, you have so. Look at your shoes.

HUGHIE: I have not been to the river.

LUCIA: Look at your shoes. There's bad men down at the river. You're not allowed down there.

HUGHIE: I have not been to the river.

LUCIA: Look at your shoes!

HUGHIE: (*Screams*) I'm looking at my shoes and I've no been to the river. (*He starts to cry*) I've not. I've no been to the river. I have not.

Lucia scrutinises him in amazement.

LUCIA: Is that you crying?

HUGHIE: Aye ... I mean, no ... I mean ... I mean ... Oh, you going to cry as well?

Lucia, on request, starts to cry: they put their arms round each other's shoulders, acknowledge the fact they are both crying and walk off together.

Scene Seven

Back shop: Two months later

Bring up accordion music, very plaintive, playing 'Santa Lucia'. It is Massimo, sitting in the back shop, wrapped in his own thoughts.

Rosinella in, coat on: pulling off a black mantilla: Lucia is with her, nice wee hat on.

ROSINELLA: She was an awfy good girl at mass today, Uncle Massimo. On you go and pick a wee sweetie, Lucia.

Lucia hovers.

ROSINELLA: Guess who was sitting right in front of us. That Bridget Devlin. On you go, Lucia.

Lucia goes, reluctantly.

ROSINELLA: Listen, Massimo, you'll need to have a word with Franco about that lassie.

MASSIMO: Rosie ...

ROSINELLA: I've tried, but he'll no listen to me.

MASSIMO: Rosinella ...

ROSINELLA: Now don't you start sticking up for him. You can start stopping covering up for him for a start. Telling his daddy he's with us when all the time he's out with HER! Bloody cheek!

Massimo puts down his accordion.

MASSIMO: Rosie, please ...

ROSINELLA: Do you know what I think? God forgive me right enough, but I think since she lost her daddy she's just using that to make Franco feel sorry for her.

MASSIMO: Rosie, there's bad news.

ROSINELLA: (*Full of fear*) No from Italy?

MASSIMO: On the radio.

ROSINELLA: (*Relief/scoffs*) See you and that radio!

MASSIMO: Rosie – we're at war.

ROSINELLA: Who is?

MASSIMO: This country's at war against Germany. It was on the radio. Oh Rosie ...

ROSINELLA: (*Soothing*) OK, so it's happened. You've been saying it would all along. But it's got nothing to do with us, Massimo. We're Italian, we just live here. It's not our country.

MASSIMO: I don't know, Rosie. Maybe you're right.

ROSINELLA: 'Course I'm right. Now come on, they'll all be in after twelve o'clock mass and the ice cream's no even on.

MASSIMO: I suppose I better get a move on.

He goes out, wearily.

Rosinella much more worried than she lets on. She goes to the door to the front shop.

ROSINELLA: (*Shouts*) Lucia!

Lucia in, eating a sweetie.

ROSINELLA: Who does your Auntie Rosinella love best in the whole wide world?

LUCIA: Me.

Rosinella looks at her adoringly and hugs her.

Scene Eight

Back shop

MASSIMO: (*Furious/incredulous*) You did what?

FRANCO: I've joined up.

MASSIMO: How could you do that?

FRANCO: I took the train into Glasgow and I –

MASSIMO: Right. OK. You got carried away. OK. I can see that. But we'll get you out of it somehow. What can we do? Go and see them, I'll come with you. Explain you're Italian and –

FRANCO: But I'm not. I was born here. That makes me British. There's no going back now. I'm telling you, I've joined up.

Massimo takes Franco's head in his two hands and shakes it gently.

MASSIMO: (*Gently*) Oh Franco, Franco, what have you done?

FRANCO: Stop treating me like an idiot, Massimo. I know what I'm doing.

MASSIMO: But why?

FRANCO: Why do you think? To get out that shop.

MASSIMO: Jesus, Mary and Joseph.

FRANCO: (*Defensive*) Well, you got out, didn't you?

MASSIMO: Aye, to sell hot pea specials and double nougats, you stupid bastard. No to get my fucking brains blown out in a fucking war that's got fuck all to do with me.

Franco glares at him, would like to hit him but calms down.

FRANCO: I don't have to answer to you. I don't have to answer to anyone. No any more.

Franco storms out: passes Rosinella on the way in.

FRANCO: (*To Rosinella*) And before you start, it's got nothing to do with you either!

Rosinella looks at Massimo, frightened.

MASSIMO: Rosinella.

ROSINELLA: I heard.

MASSIMO: I thought you might.

ROSINELLA: (*Getting quietly angry*) I heard alright.

MASSIMO: I just can't understand it.

ROSINELLA: Oh I can, Massimo. Believe me, I can.

Scene Nine

Ginger store: A week or so later

Bring up romantic music.

Franco and Bridget in, not exactly waltzing, more leaning against each other, swaying gently to the music.

FRANCO: You alright?

BRIDGET: Mmmmm.

FRANCO: You sure?

BRIDGET: Hmmmm.

FRANCO: You don't regret it then?

Bridget lifts her head from his shoulder, shakes her head: puts it back on his shoulder and snuggles in.

FRANCO: I wouldn't want you to regret it.

BRIDGET: Franco, listen to me. My mammy saw my da off to his work one morning. Never saw him alive again. I'd regret it more if anything happened to you, and we hadn't ... (*Embarrassed, she can't find the word for it*)

FRANCO: Nothing's going to happen to me, Bridget. I promise.

BRIDGET: First I lose my da. Now you're going away.

FRANCO: Ssshhhh.

BRIDGET: You know my mammy still makes up my da's piece. Every single morning. (*Pause*) We've tried telling her. (*Pause*) I don't want to end up like that.

FRANCO: You won't. I promise.

They carry on dancing: Franco starts to sing 'Parlami d'amore ...'

Scene Ten

Rosinella, Massimo, Lucia, standing waiting, very serious.

FRANCO: (*Voice from offstage: singing*) Giovinezza, giovinezza, Primavera di bellezza –

Franco in, trying to be cheery, kit bag in hand, dumps it, holds out his arms.

FRANCO: That's me. I'm off.

ROSINELLA: You sure you don't need anything?

FRANCO: I'm sure.

MASSIMO: You alright for money?

FRANCO: Aye, ma faither's seen me alright. (*A beat*) I better go, eh?

ROSINELLA: Say goodbye to your Uncle Franco, Lucia.

Franco hugs her and kisses her two cheeks.

FRANCO: You be a good girl now, you hear? And don't go kissing too many boys.

Lucia giggles.

Franco comes to Rosinella: he holds out his arms.

FRANCO: Ciao Bella.

Rosinella throws her arms round him and kisses him on both cheeks. She can't speak. He takes her two hands.

FRANCO: You better keep an eye on that daft faither of mine. Keep cutting his toenails.

She nods, he pats her hands.

Massimo is scared to look at him. He reaches Massimo, holds out his hands.

FRANCO: Fratello mio.

Massimo looks at him: he holds his hand up to Franco's face, his fingers touching each other, and shakes his hand angrily at him: then they hold each other in a strong embrace: Massimo, fighting back the tears, sings.

MASSIMO: 'Pack up your troubles in your old kit bag and smile, smile, smile ...' You might at least get the song right, you daft bastard.

Franco nods: claps Massimo on the back and goes, abruptly.

ROSINELLA: This is all wrong, Massimo. All wrong.

Massimo still trying to get himself together.

ROSINELLA: Him away there, away from his family. God only knows what he's got ahead of him. He could get blown to bits.

Massimo notices Lucia's frightened look.

MASSIMO: (*To Lucia*) Away you go and play, hen. (*To Rosinella*) You should watch what you say in front of the wean.

ROSINELLA: Somebody's put him up to this. And I think I know who she is.

MASSIMO: Nobody put him up to anything. Franco's all the man he'll ever be. (*A beat*) There's something else that frightens me.

ROSINELLA: What?

MASSIMO: Italy coming into the war. It's looking bad, Rosie.

ROSINELLA: What's that got to do with us?

MASSIMO: We're Italian, aren't we?

ROSINELLA: So what? We just live here. We're just ordinary working people.

MASSIMO: But if Italy's at war with this country –

ROSINELLA: (*Interrupting*) Italians are good for this country. Who else is prepared to work till eleven o'clock every night, eh? You tell me that. And we work for ourselves, it's no as if we take any jobs away from any Scotch people. We stick together, pay our own way, stick to the laws. What more do they want?

Hughie, arms outstretched, making aeroplane noises, comes 'flying' across the stage, making shooting noises – 'pee-aiow, pee-aiow'.

Lucia saunters in: looks at him disdainfully: he circles her, still an aeroplane.

HUGHIE: Pee-aiow, pee-aiow! Pee-aiow, pee-aiow!

Lucia continues to look at him with contempt which begins to fade as she becomes uncomfortable.

Freeze on Hughie and Lucia.

Pick up on Massimo and Rosinella.

MASSIMO: Maybe we should go back to Italy, Rosie. While we still can.

ROSINELLA: No. We've worked hard for everything we've got. We're no going to throw it all away.

Freeze on Massimo and Rosinella: pick up on Hughie and Lucia: he continues to circle her, shooting sounds getting louder.

HUGHIE: Pee-aiow, pee-aiow! Pee-aiow, pee-aiow! Pee-aiow, pee-aiow!

Lucia cowering, threatened by it.

Freeze on Hughie and Lucia: pick up on Massimo and Rosinella.

MASSIMO: I'm frightened, Rosie.

ROSINELLA: What for? Everybody likes you.

Freeze on Massimo and Rosinella: pick up on Lucia and Hughie.

He is still making shooting noises, she is still cowering: it dawns on her it is a game, she comes out of it: kicks Hughie on the shin.

LUCIA: Beat it, Hughie Devlin!

Hughie rubs his shin.

HUGHIE: I don't like this game.

LUCIA: And I don't like it either.

She struts off.

Pick up on Massimo.

MASSIMO: I've lived here since I was a wee boy. I went to school here, my brother was born here, my mammy's buried here. I always thought I was lucky. I had two countries. Now I feel I've got nowhere.

Scene Eleven

Back shop: Two months later

Rosinella making a pizza base at the table: Bridget in, looking very worried. Rosinella surprised and not very pleased to see her.

BRIDGET: I'm sorry to bother you, Mrs Pedreschi.

ROSINELLA: You're looking for your wee brother!

BRIDGET: It was you I wanted a word with, Mrs Pedreschi, if I could. Lucia said you were through here.

ROSINELLA: So, what is it you want to see me about?

BRIDGET: Franco.

ROSINELLA: (*Scoffs*) I've to laugh at you girls. You never give up, do you?

BRIDGET: Please, Mrs Pedreschi, I was hoping you could give me some news.

ROSINELLA: Oh aye, I'll give you news alright. He's no here. Went away to the war, as if you didn't know. His faither's going daft worrying about him.

BRIDGET: I thought you might know where he is.

ROSINELLA: I've hardly slept a wink since he left.

BRIDGET: I just have to know where he is. How can I get in touch with him?

ROSINELLA: What's this war got to do with him, eh? You tell me that. He's an Italian. I don't know what to think any more. My head's sore thinking.

BRIDGET: Please, Mrs Pedreschi, it's important.

ROSINELLA: What got into him, eh, made him forget where he really belongs? (*Looking directly at Bridget*) Who was it turned his head? That's what I'd like to know.

BRIDGET: Mrs Pedreschi, please ...

ROSINELLA: Please what? Don't tell me you've come to say sorry. A bit late now, isn't it?

BRIDGET: Mrs Pedreschi, I just want to know how I can get in touch with Franco. Just a letter.

Rosinella eyes her up and down.

ROSINELLA: So he took you out a couple of times. Don't think that means anything. Franco, he's Italian, he's played around a wee bit with some Scotch girls – so what? You're no the first and you'll no be the last.

BRIDGET: Franco's not like that.

ROSINELLA: Don't you kid yourself, they're all like that. I've lived here long enough and I've seen it time and time again. Do you think if Italian girls were allowed out – if they got doing all the things you girls do – do you think for one minute Franco would've looked twice at you?

Bridget almost in tears.

BRIDGET: It's not true.

ROSINELLA: Now, I'm no saying it's right but you girls bring it on yourselves.

BRIDGET: But I love Franco, Mrs Pedreschi. I need him.

ROSINELLA: (*Relenting slightly*) You just think that, hen. That's because you're still upset over your daddy. I know I sound hard, but it's for your own good I'm telling you this. You forget about Franco, you hear?

BRIDGET: Franco loves me.

ROSINELLA: (*As if annoyed at Franco*) Did he tell you that? I'm no kidding you, I love him like a brother, but he can be a right fly-boy at times. Saying things he doesn't mean, making promises he can't keep. I just hope you didn't fall for that one. Because I tell you this, hen, Italian men, they only love one girl – and that's the girl they marry.

BRIDGET: But it's ME Franco loves.

ROSINELLA: So, did he ask you to marry him?

BRIDGET: No – but –

ROSINELLA: Well – there you are then. Just you forget him, hen. Because see when this war's over, Franco will be marrying an Italian girl. Now you find yourself a nice Scotch boyfriend, you hear?

Rosinella returns to her pizza base, bashing it about, freezes Bridget out: Bridget walks away slowly.

Scene Twelve

Ginger store: The same day

MASSIMO: You got your gas mask, Lucia? You got yours, Hughie? Right. You sure you can manage, the pair of you?

HUGHIE: (*Miffed*) I thought it was supposed to be my job.

LUCIA: You said I could help, sure you did, Uncle Massimo?

MASSIMO: You know all your prices, Hughie?

HUGHIE: (*Knows it off by heart*) Pokey hats a penny and tuppence; wafers a penny and tuppence; single nugget tuppence, double nugget thruppence. No snowballs, no sponges, no flakes, no tick and plenty of Tally's Blood ... Oops, sorry Mr Pedreschi, I meant to say 'raspberry'.

MASSIMO: Now off you go the pair of you.

Watches them go affectionately.

They jostle each other for handles of the barrow.

HUGHIE: I've to push.

LUCIA: I want to push.

HUGHIE: It's my job. I always push.

LUCIA: It's my Uncle Massimo's barrow. I can push if I want.

HUGHIE: Chances each, then?

LUCIA: Alright. Me first.

She gets barrow from him and pushes ahead, he follows on, knows he's beat.

Massimo watching them, wipes his hands, laughs to himself: doesn't see Bridget creep softly in behind him.

BRIDGET: Mr Pedreschi?

Massimo turns round, surprised, but pleased to see her.

MASSIMO: Wee Bridget Devlin.

BRIDGET: Hello, Mr Pedreschi.

MASSIMO: If you're looking for Hughie you've just missed him. They're away down the Palace Grounds with the barrow.

BRIDGET: No, it's ... eh, you I wanted to see, Mr Pedreschi. If you've got a minute.

MASSIMO: (*Surprised*) Aye, right. Sure, hen.

He waits for Bridget to speak: she doesn't.

MASSIMO: I was that sorry to hear about your daddy. How's your mammy?

BRIDGET: Lost without him. (*A beat*) Mr Pedreschi – I have to ask you a favour.

MASSIMO: What is it, hen?

BRIDGET: I know I've no right to ask ...

MASSIMO: Just ask, come on.

BRIDGET: I was wondering ... could I ask you for a wee loan of some money? I hate asking – only I don't know who else – I'll pay you back sometime – honest – I just ...

MASSIMO: How much do you need, Bridget?

BRIDGET: If you could spare two pound?

Massimo takes money from trouser pocket. Bridget watches, distressed.

BRIDGET: It's just I – I – need – I'm a wee bit – I – I don't want my mammy to know ... it's just ...

MASSIMO: It's alright, hen, you don't have to explain anything to me.

BRIDGET: I'll pay you back, Mr Pedreschi. Somehow.

MASSIMO: Listen, hen, you've no to bother about paying it back, you hear? I was awfy fond of your daddy. He was a good man and I know your mammy's had it hard since he – since she lost him. Here, hen, is three pound enough?

Bridget reaches out to take it, bends over and kisses his hand. She starts to cry, her tears running on to his hand: Massimo distressed for her.

MASSIMO: Oh no, hen, come on now, come on. There's no need for that.

BRIDGET: Oh God, if my da only knew ...

MASSIMO: He'd do the same for me. Now come on, hen, I know you miss him, but you need to be strong for your mammy.

She pulls herself together.

BRIDGET: Mr Pedreschi, thank you.

MASSIMO: You alright now, hen?

Bridget nods.

MASSIMO: I'll no breathe a word to a soul.

Bridget starts to walk out, turns back.

BRIDGET: See if Italy does come into the war, Mr Pedreschi, you'll no have to worry. Everybody likes you.

Bridget goes, Massimo looks after her, sadly: carries on with his work, maybe sweeping.

MASSIMO: Ma faither's got a house in Italy. I've no been back since we got Lucia. Her daddy's supposed to look after it for us. You know what that means! It's just got the two rooms, bare walls, bare floors, and the hens march in and out all day long. There's no water, no cludgie, no lights, no gas. You've to walk two miles for water and cook on a big black pot on the fire. If you want a keigh you've to go outside. There's a hole in the ground with a plank across it and the flies buzz round your arse. (*A beat*) God, I wish I was there now.

ROSINELLA: (*Screams*) Massimo!

Massimo runs to her.

MASSIMO: (*Shouts*) Lucia!

Lucia runs up to them.

LUCIA: What's wrong?

ROSINELLA: (*To Massimo*) Shut the shop up. Quick.

Massimo rushes out to front shop: Rosinella grabs Lucia.

ROSINELLA: Lucia, my darling, I want you to do everything your Uncle Massimo says. You have to be brave. For me.

LUCIA: What's happening?

ROSINELLA: You're too wee to really understand, but Italy is in the war against this country and the people are taking it out on the Italians.

Massimo in: Lucia runs to him.

LUCIA: Uncle Massimo, I'm frightened.

MASSIMO: It's alright, darling, your Uncle Massimo's here.

ROSINELLA: Get the black-outs up quick.

MASSIMO: They're up.

ROSINELLA: We better shift some stuff. You come give me a hand, Lucia. You get the cigarettes, Massimo, take them upstairs.

Lucia and Rosinella go into front shop.

MASSIMO: Rosie, get back in here.

Rosinella and Lucia in, each carrying boxes of sweeties.

MASSIMO: What're you doing?

ROSINELLA: Get these upstairs. Quick. Hide as much as we can. They'll waste everything.

MASSIMO: No, Rosie, leave it. Let them take what they like, waste what they like. So long as they leave you two alone.

ROSINELLA: (*Shocked*) Massimo! You don't think ... surely? They'll no touch us!

Noise of brick bashing against boards: the 'mob' outside, banging on the doors and windows: shouting.

MOB: Get the Tallies! Fascist bastards!

Lucia starts to weep, frightened, Rosinella holds her, crouches with her. The level of noise increases: Massimo crouches over them, arms protectively round them.

Rosinella trying to shoosh Lucia: Massimo looking round him in despair: Rosinella putting a restraining hand on his arm.

MOB: Get the bastard.
    Waste the place.
    Fascist pigs.
    Greasy Tallies.

MASSIMO: (*Whispers*) They cannie do this to me.

ROSINELLA: (*Whispers*) Massimo ... please ... don't do
    anything. Please, please.

Jeers continue.

MOB: Come out and fight, you bastarding Tally!

ROSINELLA: Oh Sant' Antonio. San Giuseppe.

Massimo makes to go to the door.

MASSIMO: I can't just stand here and do nothing.

ROSINELLA: Massimo ... no! Don't leave us.

*She holds on to his arm as the mob breaks into front shop: we see
    their silhouettes carrying sticks and stones. We see and hear the
    smashing up and the jeers –*

MOB: Tally bastards (*etc.*).

*Rosinella, Lucia and Massimo stay huddled: Lucia buries her head
    in Rosinella's shoulder and keeps it there. Rosinella praying
    and shooshing Lucia: Massimo hovering over them protectively,
    but looking over his shoulder in direction of the front shop,
    feeling every blow: Rosinella, slowly reciting the Our Father, in
    Italian, to herself.*

The noise dies down and the mob moves on.

Massimo gets to his feet.

ROSINELLA: Stay here.

MASSIMO: I need to go. I need to see what they've done to my shop.

He goes: Lucia still can't look.

LUCIA: Have they gone away? Have they gone away?

ROSINELLA: (*Very soothing*) It's alright, it's alright, it's all over. They're away. See – they're away. Look, there's Uncle Massimo.

Massimo returns, looking defeated.

MASSIMO: Eight years' work gone in eight minutes.

LUCIA: They'll not come back, will they?

Loud banging at door again: Lucia screams.

They jump back into their huddle, heads down.

Banging continues, insistent.

VOICE FROM OFFSTAGE: Massimo Pedreschi!

They crouch: no reply.

VOICE FROM OFFSTAGE: Massimo Pedreschi!

No reply.

VOICE FROM OFFSTAGE: Massimo Pedreschi! Open up.
    This is the police.

MASSIMO: Oh, thank God.

ROSINELLA: Go let them in. Quick.

Massimo goes: Lucia tries to grab him.

LUCIA: Uncle Massimo, stay here.

MASSIMO: It's alright, hen.

He goes.

ROSINELLA: It's alright, hen, I told you it's alright. The police
    are here. They'll catch the bad men. It's all over now. It's
    all finished. All gone.

LUCIA: Auntie Rosinella.

ROSINELLA: What, darling?

LUCIA: See my daddy in Italy? Is he in the war?

Massimo, shattered, in from front shop.

MASSIMO: They're taking me in, Rosie.

ROSINELLA: I'll come with you. Give a statement.

MASSIMO: No, you don't understand, I'm being arrested.

ROSINELLA: Arrested? You? Ma, what've you done?

MASSIMO: I'm a ... Tally.

ROSINELLA: What about the pigs that did this to our shop? How can they no take them in, leave you here?

MASSIMO: I better just go.

ROSINELLA: No, you cannie go. You cannie leave me. Us two, on our own? With that lot out there?

MASSIMO: I have to Rosie. The police are waiting for me.

ROSINELLA: Where? Out there?

MASSIMO: Yes.

ROSINELLA: I'll soon fix them.

Rosinella heads for the door to front shop: Massimo stands in her way.

MASSIMO: Rosie, please. I'll just go.

ROSINELLA: What's to happen? You'll be back tonight or what?

MASSIMO: They'll tell me nothing. Better get in touch with the lawyer. And don't worry. If we do as we're told we'll be alright. (*A beat*) Oh Rosie.

He hugs her and goes.

Scene Thirteen

Ginger store: Two weeks later

Lucia and Hughie fixing ginger boxes to play at schools.

Lucia in charge: Hughie reluctant.

HUGHIE: You got going the teacher the last time.

LUCIA: Whose Uncle Massimo's ginger boxes are they?

HUGHIE: (*Resigned*) Yours.

Lucia picks up something to use as a pointer.

LUCIA: Right, sit up straight. Fold your arms.

Hughie obliges.

LUCIA: Two and two?

HUGHIE: Four.

LUCIA: Three and two?

HUGHIE: Five.

LUCIA: Six and three?

HUGHIE: Nine. I mean eight. No, nine, I mean.

LUCIA: Seven and five?

HUGHIE: Eh ... Eh ... That's a hard one.

LUCIA: It's not hard for all the other wee boys and girls. Is it, boys and girls? Seven and five?

Hughie starts counting on his fingers.

LUCIA: Come on, come on, seven and five? He's not doing very well, is he boys and girls?

HUGHIE: Seven and five?

LUCIA: You heard.

Pokes him with pointer.

HUGHIE: Seven ADD ON five you mean?

LUCIA: You heard.

Pokes him with pointer.

Hughie trying to count on fingers, mouthing figures, gets to 'seven' then to 'ten'. Lucia makes him lose count: jabs him with her pointer.

LUCIA: Too long! I can't spend all day with one child. I've got all these other little children to see to as well, you know. Little SCOTTISH boys and girls. I think they deserve some of the teacher's time too. You should have done these sums last night, Franco. Why didn't you?

HUGHIE: Eh, well, I forgot.

LUCIA: Oh, you 'forgot', did you? Do you hear that, boys and girls? Little Franco 'forgot'. Sure you weren't too busy serving the shop?

HUGHIE: No, miss.

LUCIA: Or maybe you don't have pencils in your house. Or maybe you don't have a house. Have you got a house?

HUGHIE: Yes, miss.

LUCIA: No use telling fibs, now, is it, Franco? We all know you live in a shop. Now don't laugh boys and girls. It's not Franco's fault he lives in a shop.

HUGHIE: Twelve.

LUCIA: Oh, so there's twelve of you living there. My oh my! Not all in the same bed I hope. Now stop laughing, boys and girls, it's not funny.

HUGHIE: Seven and five is twelve.

LUCIA: Oh, you're too late now. I don't know what you're doing in this class in the first place. A little ruffian like you. A sleekit little, greasy little, smelly little ...

It's gone too far. Hughie jumps up, knocks away his ginger box.

HUGHIE: I don't like this game.

LUCIA: Well, I don't like it either.

They are staring at each other: it is broken by Rosinella's screams.

ROSINELLA: (*Voice from offstage*) Lucia! Lucia!

Rosinella, highly distraught, clutching a newspaper, in back shop: Lucia and Hughie run to her: she thrusts the paper at them.

ROSINELLA: Lucia, Lucia, what's it say? What's it say? Tell me what it says. (*Blessing herself*) Oh, Sant' Antonio, San Giuseppe. Oh no, don't tell me. Oh, Massimo, Massimo!

The children spread out paper on the table.

LUCIA: Where?

Rosinella points wildly to the paper.

ROSINELLA: Something about a ship.

Hughie and Lucia try to read the report: Rosinella in background going spare: blessing herself and repeating 'San Giuseppe, Sant' Antonio'.

Lucia and Hughie study the paper.

LUCIA: It says 'ship' there.

HUGHIE: 'T. O. R – tor'

LUCIA: 'P' – 'Torp'... something.

HUGHIE: I've got it. 'Torpedo'.

LUCIA: A ship got torpedoed.

ROSINELLA: Oh, San Guiseppe.

LUCIA: What's that word?

HUGHIE: 'En ... En ... En ...'. Something ... 'my'.

LUCIA: 'Enemy'.

HUGHIE: 'Italians' – I know that word.

LUCIA: K. K – I. K – I – L – L. 'Kill–'

HUGHIE: 'Killed'.

Rosinella grabs the paper.

ROSINELLA: Give me that! (*She looks at it helplessly. She can't read*) What about your Uncle Massimo? Does it say he was on that ship? See if it says who was on that ship. Oh Massimo, Massimo!

Hughie takes paper and stumbles with words.

HUGHIE: 'At six o'clock this morning a British ship', something 'Italian and other enemy aliens, was torpedoed.' You mean your Uncle Massimo was on that ship?

ROSINELLA: Nothing. I've heard nothing. I've no seen my man since they took him out of here. (*Near hysterics*) Oh marito mio. Marito mio è morto. È vero, vero, vero. È morto.

Lucia starts to cry, frightened: this pulls Rosinella up, forces her to calm down.

HUGHIE: It says it's called the 'Ar – an – do – ra Star'. The 'Arandora Star'.

LUCIA: Auntie Rosinella, what about his daddy? They took him too, didn't they?

ROSINELLA: (*Fresh worry*) Oh my God, daddy! Surely to God no him! (*A beat*) Wait a minute, did you say 'enemies'?

HUGHIE: It says here … 'enemy aliens' …

ROSINELLA: (*Hope returning*) That cannie mean Massimo. Surely. Your Uncle Massimo's no an 'enemy', eh Lucia? (*To Lucia*) They must be OK, eh? I mean, they're no 'enemies'.

Rosinella takes money from her purse and hands it to Lucia.

ROSINELLA: Here, Lucia, take this. I want you to go to the chapel and light a candle for all the souls that were on that ship, and pray to God your Uncle Massimo wasn't one of them.

LUCIA: I thought you said –

ROSINELLA: (*Interrupting*) Just do it, Lucia.

ROSINELLA: (*Blesses herself*) Eternal rest grant unto them, O Lord, and let perpetual light shine upon them, may they rest in peace, Amen.

Scene Fourteen

Same day: Candlestand/church

Lucia lighting candle and putting it on the stand beside other lit candles: she kneels and prays.

While this is going on Massimo appears, framed by the candlelight.

MASSIMO: When they lifted us that night I'd two or three pound in my pocket. That's one thing ma faither always drummed into us. Spent the night in the cell with the other Italians they'd lifted. There was old Albert Cipoline. Poor old bugger couldn't stop crying, wouldn't let me out his sight. The last I'd seen him he was playing bowls with ma faither down at the Palace Grounds. Never missed a Tuesday. Next morning they put us on these trucks and took us to a camp in Edinburgh. The worst of it was we couldn't get anybody to tell us anything. Rosinella sent Mr Galbraith to see me. She was outside but they wouldn't let her in. I kept asking for news of ma faither but nobody would tell us anything. I don't know how many days passed before they put us on a train. Turned out it was going to Bury. They'd turned an Old Mill into a camp and were filling it up with Italians from all over the place, and it was the same story I heard over and over again. This one got his café smashed up – that one's left seven or eight weans and he's showing us their pictures. Another one's got his sons fighting in the British army and someone else is frightened for his family back in Italy. Me – I was frantic for news of ma faither. But I was trying not to think. That's what got me through. If I thought about what was going to happen to us – I just got scared. If I thought about Rosinella ... (*Stops. His voice catches*) So I tried to keep thinking about my shop. How I was going to fix it up again, back the way it was. It was never fancy, mind you, but always nice and clean. And I kept looking for ma faither.

Finally, this day, he turns up. He'd been picked up in Glasgow, kept in Barlinnie, then sent down here, to wait with the rest of us. You know the first thing he says to me? 'Who's minding the bloody shop?' He was an awfy swearer, ma faither. I says, 'Who do you think? Rosinella.' He says, 'She'll be looking after mine as well. It's bloody stupid anyway, having two bloody shops in the one bloody family.' I had to laugh, I says, 'Dad, how can you worry about that at a time like this?' He says, 'What the bloody hell d'you want me to do? Lie down and let the bastards shoot me?' He was an awfy swearer, ma faither. No use arguing with him. Twisted auld bugger, so he was.

Then one morning these officers come in, set themselves up at this big table at one end of the room and one of them starts reading names off a list. He calls 'Stasio Pedreschi' and I goes forward with ma faither but the soldier says to me, 'Wait till you're called.' I says, 'But that's ma faither' – he says, 'Stand back. Wait till you're called.' He tries to push ma faither into the line but ma faither is holding on to ma arm. I can still feel his nails digging into me, he was holding on that tight. I says, 'You cannie split us up. He's ma faither. Let me go with him.' He says, 'Wait till you're called. Now stand back, please.' I looked at ma faither. He was that wee looking. I'd to wrench his hand off my arm. 'You see and behave yourself, auld yin,' I says, 'and watch that tongue of yours.' He says to me, 'You alright for money, son?' Next thing I know they're marching them out and my name still hasn't been called.

A couple of days later they came for the rest of us. Took us to Liverpool docks and piled us on the SS *Ettrick*. Wouldn't tell us where they were taking us. I didn't know, before I left, what had happened to ma faither.

Lucia lights another candle and gets to her feet, hands it to Massimo and goes.

MASSIMO: *Arandora Star*. Non vi scorderemo mai.

He puts the candle on the stand.

MASSIMO: We will never forget you.

Scene Fifteen

Ginger Store: 1943

HUGHIE: (*Up to Lucia*) You sure you want to become blood-brothers?

LUCIA: Sure I'm sure. You got the knife?

HUGHIE: That was my daddy's penknife. Where do you do it?

LUCIA: On the thumb ... Your 'thumb', I said.

HUGHIE: Give me your hand.

LUCIA: You go first.

HUGHIE: What, cut myself you mean?

LUCIA: Yes.

HUGHIE: My own self?

LUCIA: Yes.

HUGHIE: Right. OK. You're sure?

Lucia covers her eyes, Hughie nips himself with the knife, sees his blood, sucks his thumb, but is delighted with himself.

HUGHIE: Done it.

LUCIA: (*Worried*) You did?

HUGHIE: Your go.

LUCIA: Wait a wee minute.

HUGHIE: Come on, it's no sore. No really.

LUCIA: Just give me a wee minute.

HUGHIE: What for?

LUCIA: Just to get ready.

Hughie grabs her hand and puts knife up to it.

HUGHIE: It's dead easy. Just do it.

LUCIA: (*Hysterics*) Oh mammy-daddy ... Mammy-daddy, no, no, no.

Hughie stops.

HUGHIE: What is it?

LUCIA: It's too sore. It's too sore.

HUGHIE: I never even touched you. Just close your eyes, you'll hardly feel it.

She closes her eyes, turns away.

LUCIA: Alright, I'm ready now.

The moment he touches her with the knife, hysterics start.

LUCIA: Oh mammy-daddy, mammy-daddy – stop stop stop.

HUGHIE: Something wrong?

LUCIA: I can't do it.

HUGHIE: Oh, that's great. After all I've been through. I've shed my blood for you.

Lucia examines his thumb.

LUCIA: (*With contempt*) You can't even see it.

HUGHIE: There, it's there.

LUCIA: Where?

HUGHIE: There.

LUCIA: I don't see any blood.

HUGHIE: Well, it's stopped bleeding now, hasn't it? You've took that long.

He is annoyed, plonks himself down.

HUGHIE: Women!

He takes bottle of ginger, takes a gulp: she holds out her hand and he gives it to her. She sits down.

LUCIA: I did want to do it, honest, Hughie.

She takes a gulp and hands it back.

HUGHIE: You'd think you were a wee baby.

He takes a gulp and hands it back. Lucia takes a sip, watching him, passes it back.

LUCIA: Couldn't we just – you know – kid on we done it? We could still call ourselves blood-brothers.

HUGHIE: No. You've wasted it.

LUCIA: Who would know? It's supposed to be a secret anyway.

HUGHIE: It's not the same as mixing your blood.

He takes a gulp and hands it back.

LUCIA: Listen. I've got a great idea. We can do it with the ginger.

HUGHIE: How?

LUCIA: If I take a slug and spit it back in – then you take a slug and spit it back in – then I take another slug. And we'll mix it all up.

HUGHIE: Do you think it will still take?

LUCIA: Yes. I'll go first this time.

He watches her as she performs her bit, then he follows suit, with her watching every move. He hands it back and she drinks.

LUCIA: That's it done.

HUGHIE: So what are we now then?

LUCIA: I suppose I must be your ... ?

HUGHIE: Slever-sister.

LUCIA: (*Appalled*) No. No, I'm your 'ginger-sister'.

HUGHIE: And I'm your 'ginger-brother'.

LUCIA: For ever.

HUGHIE: And ever.

LUCIA: Amen.

A reverent hush: Hughie breaks it.

HUGHIE: My bum's still sore.

LUCIA: I'm sorry, Hughie. Honest.

HUGHIE: What did you have to tell them it was my birthday for?

LUCIA: I didn't. They caught me making your birthday card.

HUGHIE: Thirteen bumps.

LUCIA: How come?

HUGHIE: Nine for my birthday, one for good luck, one for bad luck, one for Christmas, one for Easter.

LUCIA: My Uncle Massimo's missed two of my birthdays now. I think he's never coming home.

HUGHIE: You've no to say things like that, Lucia.

LUCIA: Well my Uncle Franco's never coming home. And my Auntie Rosinella cries all the time.

HUGHIE: So does our Bridget.

Scene Sixteen

Pedreschi's back shop: A week later

Rosinella ironing on table. Bridget in.

ROSINELLA: Bridget.

BRIDGET: Hello, Mrs Pedreschi.

ROSINELLA: You heard about Franco?

BRIDGET: That's why I'm here.

ROSINELLA: That was good of you.

Rosinella puts down her iron, gets hanky from up her sleeve and wipes her eyes.

ROSINELLA: I don't know how much more I can take.

Bridget gently touches her arm.

BRIDGET: I have to show you something.

ROSINELLA: Twenty-three year old. How's Massimo going to take this? That's him lost his faither – now his brother.

BRIDGET: How is he – Mr Pedreschi?

ROSINELLA: Still in Canada. The lawyer keeps trying to get him home, but we'll need to wait and see.

BRIDGET: Mrs Pedreschi, I have to speak to you. It's important. I got a letter from Franco.

ROSINELLA: A letter. How can that be? What you saying? They've made a mistake? Oh please God, they've made a mistake.

BRIDGET: Oh no, Mrs Pedreschi, there's no mistake. Franco wrote this the night before he went into that battle – to be posted in the event of his ...

Bridget sits down, gets letter out of her bag, she handles it with tenderness/reverence: looks at the first page very lovingly, and goes to the second.

BRIDGET: He asked me to come to see you ... This part here. It's about you. (*She tries to hand it to Rosinella but Rosinella hesitates*) Do you want me to read it out? 'Tell Rosinella and Lucia how much I love them. Tell Lucia she has to work hard and do well at school. Tell them they were in my thoughts up till the last. Tell Rosinella not to grieve too much for me. What has happened is the will of our Blessed Lord. When Massimo gets home tell him he has to be strong and carry on. I will be with my father in heaven. No doubt he is still moaning and groaning and annoying all the saints.'

Rosinella manages a wee laugh, despite the tears: Bridget kisses the letter and fold it and puts it in her envelope.

They sit in silence for a moment, then Rosinella gets a thought.

ROSINELLA: Why did he send it to you?

BRIDGET: (*Too upset to answer*) I ...

ROSINELLA: I wonder why he sent it to you?

BRIDGET: You really don't know, do you?

ROSINELLA: It must be because he knows I cannie read.

Rosinella turns away.

Bridget looks at her in disbelief.

Scene Seventeen

Back shop: Late 1944

Rosinella up to Lucia with a half-made long white dress, helps her into it and starts to pin it.

Lucia yawns.

ROSINELLA: I know it's late, hen, but I'm nearly finished. You're lovely in it so you are. I'll cut the lace off this wee party dress and make a nice collar out it. You mind this?

LUCIA: You got me it just before I started school.

ROSINELLA: It's not what I would have wanted for your Confirmation but I'll make it up to you. Here, try on the veil.

Rosinella helps her with it, fixes her hair etc.

ROSINELLA: If only your Uncle Massimo could be here to see it.

LUCIA: Is my Uncle Massimo never coming back?

ROSINELLA: Don't say things like that, my darling, of course he's coming back.

LUCIA: When?

ROSINELLA: Soon. It'll be soon.

LUCIA: That's what you always say.

ROSINELLA: That's four years, Lucia. Four years. But one of these days he'll walk through that door – and it'll be all over. We've got to keep telling ourselves that.

LUCIA: Auntie Rosinella.

ROSINELLA: Mmmm?

LUCIA: Do you think I'll ever see my daddy in Italy again?

By now Rosinella has finished putting the veil on Lucia and is preoccupied with it. She stands back and looks at her and gets the hanky out to wipe her eyes.

LUCIA: What's wrong?

ROSINELLA: You look just like a wee bride. I'm telling you this now, Lucia Ianelli, some day I'll give you a wedding, I'll give you a wedding like nobody here has ever seen before.

LUCIA: (*Enthusiastic*) Just like yours?

ROSINELLA: (*Cagey*) I didn't have much of a wedding, hen. We were awfy poor in they days.

LUCIA: (*Sympathetic*) Oh, Auntie Rosinella.

ROSINELLA: No, don't get me wrong. I wouldn't change your Uncle Massimo for any film star. No for Humphrey Bogart, no for Victor Mature. My faither wanted me to marry someone else, you know.

LUCIA: (*Enjoying it*) He did not.

ROSINELLA: (*Getting into it*) He did that. Ferdinando. He'd it all fixed up with Ferdinand's faither. He wasn't very good-looking, Ferdinand, but all the girls were after him because he had a beautiful big piece of land. That's what it's all about over there, you know. The man's got to have land. So my daddy was that pleased when his daddy picked me. It was all set. Then I met your Uncle Massimo. I must have met him when he was a wean, before him and his faither moved to Scotland, but I don't remember. I'm no kidding you, Lucia, I knew the minute I looked at him that he was for me. He was that handsome.

LUCIA: (*Disbelief*) My Uncle Massimo?

ROSINELLA: That was before he put the weight on. And he'd much more hair then and it was shining black. Nero. Nero. Oh Massimo! Swept me off ma feet he did. Oh hen, I shouldn't be telling you this ...

LUCIA: (*Desperate to hear the rest*) Oh no, go on, Auntie Rosinella.

ROSINELLA: Well, I never married Ferdinand. I married your Uncle Massimo instead. That's why I didn't have much of a wedding. (*A beat: she is deciding whether to tell her or not, then does so, with glee.*) We ran away.

LUCIA: (*Impressed*) You did not!

ROSINELLA: (*Enjoying it now*) We did. You see, in Italy, where we come from anyway, if a boy and a girl stay out together all night, then they must get married. It's true. We planned it and we did it. My faither locked me in my room because I said I wasn't going to marry Ferdinand and your Uncle Massimo came with a ladder and stole me out the window.

LUCIA: (*Laughing*) He did not!

ROSINELLA: Without a word of a lie, sure as God is my judge standing here. We just had to spend one night together, on our own. But we had nowhere to go so we hid up a tree. And we could hear them out looking for us, all round the village, calling our names and chapping all the doors. My daddy was screaming and shouting at the top of his voice and calling me for everything. And the next morning the priest rang the bell – (*She mimics the sound*) 'Do-ing, Do-ing, Do-ing' – the way he does when someone has died, to let everyone in the village know I'd disgraced my name and brought shame on my whole family. Oh it was lovely, so it was.

Banging on door in front shop: they jump in fright, automatically cower: Rosinella grabs Lucia's hand.

ROSINELLA: (*Whispers*) Who's that at this time?

LUCIA: You want me to go and see?

Rosinella restrains her: banging persists.

ROSINELLA: Ssshhh. Stay still, they'll go away.

Banging persists.

ROSINELLA: (*Shouts*) Who is it?

MASSIMO: (*Voice from offstage*) It's Massimo.

ROSINELLA: (*Screams*) Massimo!

Runs out to front shop: Lucia waits, takes off her veil, listening to their reunion: Rosinella fumbling with the door, crying.

ROSINELLA: (*Voice from offstage*) Massimo, I can't get the door. I can't get the door, Massimo. Just wait. I can't get the door.

Noise of door opening.

ROSINELLA: Oh, grazie Dio.

Lucia waits in silence.

Rosinella holds open the flaps of the doorway and Massimo comes in. Rosinella stands at doorway watching. Massimo stops and opens his arms at the sight of Lucia.

MASSIMO: Lucia?

Lucia is shy.

ROSINELLA: Kiss your Uncle Massimo, Lucia.

Lucia runs into his arms: he holds her and holds out his other arm to include Rosinella: he holds them both looking from one to the other.

MASSIMO: (*Struggling for words*) ... Nothing ... Nothing ...

He is trying to say 'Nothing will ever part us again' but he can't get it out: Rosinella understands: she puts his head on her shoulder.

ROSINELLA: It's alright. It's alright.

END OF ACT ONE

Tally's Blood
Act Two

Italian pronunciation guide

Names

Lucia	loo–<u>chee</u>–a
Luigi	loo–<u>eej</u>–ay
Pedreschi	paid–<u>rays</u>–key
Ianelli	yan–<u>ell</u>–ee

Act Two

Scene One	*cervaro*	cher–<u>var</u>–oh
	giachetta	jack–<u>ate</u>–a
	scozzese	scott–<u>says</u>–ay
	pantaloni	pant–a–<u>lone</u>–ee
Scene Eleven	*scorpione*	scorp–<u>ee–own</u>–ay
	attenzione	a–ten–zee–<u>own</u>–ay
Scene Thirteen	*piglia una sedia*	<u>peel</u>–ya oona <u>said</u>–ya
	come si chiama?	<u>comb</u>–ay see <u>kyam</u>–a?
	sole	<u>saul</u>–ay
	molto	<u>mole</u>–toe
	manegia la miseria	man–<u>edge</u>–a la mis–<u>er</u>–ee–a

Scene One

Italy: 1955

Luigi is standing at a table, looking through the contents of a case.

Massimo has just been looking over his father's house for the first time since before the war. He is moved to tears. Luigi puts an arm round his shoulder and claps him on the back.

LUIGI: Va bene, Massimo?

Massimo takes out his hanky, blows his nose, wipes his eyes.

MASSIMO: Scusa. Sorry.

Luigi shrugs.

MASSIMO: From the minute I heard what had happened to ma faither I've thought about this house. He always spoke about coming back here to live one day. I'm going to clean it up, make it nice, the way he would have like it.

LUIGI: Look over there. Look at Monte Cassino. You see that?

MASSIMO: I do, aye.

LUIGI: You see what they did to that?

MASSIMO: I know.

LUIGI: You passed through Cassino on your way here?

MASSIMO: I did, aye.

LUIGI: What's left of Cassino? You tell me that. Every single street – (*Makes exploding noise*) – La Basilica di Monte Cassino – all the villages all round about – Sant' Elia, Olivello, Capo d'Acqua …

MASSIMO: San Michele, Cervaro, Villa d'Attina …

LUIGI: (*Makes exploding noise*) Your house is still standing.

MASSIMO: You're right, Luigi.

LUIGI: I lost my olives, my pigs, my hens, my grapes …

Massimo goes into the case.

MASSIMO: I've got some things from Rosinella. There's some things for your boys.

LUIGI: Grazie.

MASSIMO: Some dresses for your wife. Some tea. Come si dice in Italian – some 'shortbread' –

LUIGI: Che è? – Short-e-bread?

MASSIMO: Eh … biscotti scozzesi.

LUIGI: Ah, biscotti scozzesi. Va bene.

MASSIMO: Cigarettes.

LUIGI: Sigarette scozzesi. 'Cap-i-stan!' Mi piace. Grazie.

Massimo takes off jacket: dumps it on table: wipes head with hanky, turns to look at the house, Luigi puts on the jacket.

MASSIMO: God this heat. (*A beat*) You know, Luigi, a good clean-out, open up the shutters, let the air through – I think I'll just sleep here tonight.

Turns round, sees Luigi with jacket.

LUIGI: Giacca scozzese.

MASSIMO: Aye.

Luigi preens/feels material.

LUIGI: È bella stoffa.

Massimo sighs.

MASSIMO: Just you have it, Luigi ...

LUIGI: (*Feigning surprise*) Oh, grazie.

MASSIMO: Prego.

Massimo takes wallet from the jacket pocket.

MASSIMO: Scusa.

LUIGI: Prego. Prego.

MASSIMO: I've brought you a picture.

Luigi looks at it.

LUIGI: Lucia?

MASSIMO: She's like her mammy, isn't she?

LUIGI: Mia piccoletta. My wee girl.

MASSIMO: No so wee now.

LUIGI: She's a good girl?

MASSIMO: Oh aye.

LUIGI: Works hard?

MASSIMO: (*Dubious*) We-ell ...

LUIGI: (*Looking at photo*) È bella. È bella, veramente.

MASSIMO: Oh aye, veramente.

Massimo holds out hand for photo, Luigi pockets it. Massimo shrugs.

MASSIMO: I'm sorry I couldn't bring her to see you this
time. Maybe in a couple of years. (*Looks back at house*)
Could I get a couple of your boys to give me a hand, do
you think?

*Massimo sweltering in the heat, loosens his shirt sleeves and collar:
Luigi gets his eye on Massimo's shirt – feels the material of
collar.*

LUIGI: Camicia scozzese?

MASSIMO: Aye, I suppose it must be.

LUIGI: È bella stoffa, no?

Massimo sighs, takes it off.

MASSIMO: Here. Try it on.

Luigi, putting on and buttoning shirt, looking into distance.

LUIGI: It breaks my heart every time I look over at Monte
    Cassino. The army had sent me up north, so I wasn't
    even here. My wife's father came and took her and
    my sons and they went up into the hills. They saw the
    planes lighting up the sky. They heard the bombs falling
    and the buildings crashing down and they didn't know
    if our house would still be there when they came down.
    And I wasn't even here.

Massimo puts an arm round his shoulder.

MASSIMO: Terrible times, Luigi, for all of us. But they're
    behind us now, eh?

LUIGI: I lost my olives, my pigs, my hens, my grapes ... (*A
    beat: gets his eye on Massimo's trousers, feels them*) Pantaloni
    scozzesi? È bella stoffa.

MASSIMO: No way, Luigi. These are the only pair I've got.

LUIGI: That's alright, Massimo. I'll swop you mine.

Starts to loosen his trousers.

Scene Two

Scotland: A few months later: Pedreschi's back shop

Bring up 'One for the money, two for the show ...' Enter Hughie and Lucia jiving to 'Blue suede shoes': obvious they are well practised, very good at it: after a bit.

LUCIA: That's my Uncle Massimo's juke box.

HUGHIE: I know.

They dance some more: then talk.

LUCIA: All the money it makes is for me.

HUGHIE: I know.

LUCIA: For when I go to Italy to visit my daddy.

HUGHIE: You told me.

They dance some more: then talk.

HUGHIE: Have you asked your Auntie Rosinella yet?

LUCIA: About Saturday?

HUGHIE: Aye.

LUCIA: Not yet.

HUGHIE: You going to ask her?

LUCIA: I said I was.

HUGHIE: What do you think she'll say?

LUCIA: She'll say no.

HUGHIE: What'll you do then?

LUCIA: I'll ask my Uncle Massimo.

HUGHIE: What if he says no?

LUCIA: (*Confident: her answer to everything*) I'll just cry.

They dance: right into it: Rosinella in background from front shop,
watches them, thoroughly enjoying it: they don't see her: record
stops: she claps.

ROSINELLA: Brava! Brava! (*Sings*) 'Blue blue – blue suede
shoes' … I like that one. I'm all going when I hear that
one. Put it on one more time, Lucia. I thought this was
your night off, Hughie.

HUGHIE: I'll … just … give Mr Pedreschi a hand to close up.

Takes trays and goes to front shop, passes Massimo on way in with
shop drawings (in till tray).

MASSIMO: 'Blood – blood – bloody suede shoes …'
If I hear that bloody song one more time I'll smash that
bloody juke box. They're writing songs about SHOES
now. What next?

ROSINELLA: (*Good-natured: punches him*) Oh, see him! You'll need to let your Uncle Massimo see the way you do the jiving, Lucia. She looks lovely so she does. Her hair swinging about her face. You get to see her lovely legs when she birrels about. And her eyes are all lit up and she's smiling. I wish Silvio Palombo could see you. How come you never danced that way with him at the Ice Cream dance, eh? Too shy, eh?

MASSIMO: I don't know who's worse. Here. Count this.

Rosinella and Lucia sit down at table and start to count the money. Hughie in and out in background with trays from front shop: then with brush and shovel, then mop and pail: working hard.

ROSINELLA: You like Silvio Palombo, don't you?

LUCIA: He's OK.

ROSINELLA: Nice-looking boy too.

LUCIA: He's OK.

ROSINELLA: Oh come on, Lucia, you can't kid me on. I know you're daft for him. But I like the way you kind of stand back a bit, don't let him see you're keen. Italian boys like that.

LUCIA: Auntie Rosinella ... ?

ROSINELLA: He cannie keep his eyes off you. And if he's who you want, then it's not for me to stand in your way. But I told his mother. I made sure I told her. 'Mrs Palombo,' I said, 'our Lucia's a lady, she's not been brought up to work in a shop, running after some man.' I tell you, Lucia, she liked me for that. They've got class, that family.

LUCIA: Auntie Rosinella ...?

ROSINELLA: I hear them all the time. 'Ma lassie's an awfy good worker' – 'Ma lassie cleaned four chickens' – I promised myself, my Lucia's to marry a man that really loves HER – no to put her in a shop and make her work. How much you got there?

LUCIA: Three pounds, seven and tenpence ha'penny.

ROSINELLA: That's what I want for you – a good life, with a good Italian man – here.

LUCIA: Auntie Rosinella.

ROSINELLA: You see the way the Italians are getting on now, eh? Beginning to make a wee bit money? Because they're prepared to WORK, that's why. I don't know anybody works so hard as the Italian men.

Hughie in: with pail and mop.

HUGHIE: That's the tables cleared and the front shop mopped, Mrs Pedreschi, and the chip pan cleaned out. Is the milk boiled?

ROSINELLA: Should be.

She turns attention back to Lucia, Hughie lifts pot from stove and pours contents into two pails: he covers them and sets them aside, working like a Trojan.

ROSINELLA: And the way they love their families. Nobody loves their families like the Italians. You want to stay for a wee bit pasta, Hughie? It's your favourite. Rigatoni.

HUGHIE: No thanks, Mrs Pedreschi. I better get up the road. Bridget's going out and I don't like my mammy left on her own.

ROSINELLA: Bridget's going out, is she? Don't tell me she's winching?

HUGHIE: No. Her and Davie are going up to Charmaine's the night – to go over all the arrangements. My mammy's no up to it.

ROSINELLA: That's right. When's the wedding now?

Hughie and Lucia exchange glances: he makes gesture of 'go ahead' to her. Lucia shakes head.

HUGHIE: Saturday.

ROSINELLA: Is he no getting married a wee bit quick, your brother?

Hughie shrugs/a bit embarrassed: Lucia mortified at Rosinella.

ROSINELLA: And where are they going to stay?

HUGHIE: At Charmaine's.

ROSINELLA: It's funny that, isn't it, but that's the way they do it here. In Italy, the girl must go to her husband's house. That's why you must have land if you've got sons.

Massimo in.

ROSINELLA: So, that'll be your mammy left with her eldest and her youngest, eh? I don't see your Bridget ever marrying, do you? You see, Lucia, there's a lot of women Bridget's age no married. The war killed that many young men. I'm right there, amn't I, Massimo?

MASSIMO: You got those pails ready, son?

HUGHIE: I'll bring them through.

MASSIMO: And give's a hand to put these shutters up before you go.

Hughie and Massimo out: Rosinella watches him go.

ROSINELLA: I'm right about that Davie, amn't I, Lucia? Give it five or six months, Hughie'll be telling us he's an uncle again. Mind you, I suppose his mother must feel it, right enough. Can you find me a wee envelope hen, a wee poke or something? What was I saying ... ah yes ... see what I mean about Italian men? Just take that brother of Hughie's. Getting married on Saturday, give him two or three days and he'll be out DRINKING with his pals.

Rosinella shooshes up when Hughie comes in, followed by Massimo: all locked up.

Massimo takes off his apron, reaches for a bottle of wine.

MASSIMO: Thanks, Hughie son. You want a wee glass of wine?

HUGHIE: I better no, Mr Pedreschi. I better get up the road.

ROSINELLA: Hang on a minute, son. (*She has slipped a couple of notes into the poke, gives it to Hughie*) Here, give this to your brother from me. Instead of a present. Help them out a wee bit, eh? (*Hughie hangs back, embarrassed*) ... Take it.

HUGHIE: Right. I'll away then.

Hughie goes.

MASSIMO: So, Lucia, you lost your tongue the night or what?

ROSINELLA: (*Launches in/verbal assault*) I was just telling her what a lucky girl she is to have Silvio Palombo after her. A fine boy, isn't he, Massimo? A good, good family too. A great business they've got. I know there's some think a hairdresser is a wee bit – a wee bit 'kinky-boy' – but they make plenty of money – and she'll get a free hairdo any time she wants.

MASSIMO: (*To Rosinella*) I see you've no lost yours. (*i.e. her tongue*)

(*Good-natured banter between Massimo and Rosinella*)

ROSINELLA: Away you go, you! The best thing ever happened to you was the day you met me. Isn't that right, Lucia?

MASSIMO: Don't listen to her, Lucia. I could've had my pick. The lassies were all crazy about me.

ROSINELLA: Oh, that's right. And I'm supposed to be that lucky you picked me – is that it?

MASSIMO: Picked her? Honest to God, Lucia, she was tripping me up. I was that handsome, she just took one look at me and what did she do? Go on, Rosie, tell her. Tell her what you did. Go on.

ROSINELLA: I fainted.

MASSIMO: That's how she got me. She banged her head when she fell down and I felt that sorry for her.

LUCIA: Auntie Rosinella, I want to ask you something.

ROSINELLA: What is it, my darling?

LUCIA: You'll say no.

MASSIMO: No, she'll no.

LUCIA: Yes, she will.

ROSINELLA: What is it? Ask me.

LUCIA: (*Goes coy*) Och no, you'll say no.

ROSINELLA: I won't.

LUCIA: Yes, you will.

MASSIMO: No, she won't.

LUCIA: Yes, she will.

ROSINELLA: What is it you want? Just ask me. You want a new dress? You want a new pair of shoes? What?

LUCIA: I want to go to the wedding with Hughie.

Stunned silence.

ROSINELLA: You what?

LUCIA: Hughie's brother's wedding on Saturday. Hughie's asked me to go with him.

ROSINELLA: He asked you – to go with HIM!

LUCIA: Yes. Can I go?

ROSINELLA: The cheek of him!

MASSIMO: Steady on, Rosie.

ROSINELLA: Who does he think he is, anyway?

LUCIA: Please, Auntie Rosinella?

ROSINELLA: And you've got some nerve to ask, lady.

LUCIA: Does that mean no?

ROSINELLA: Fine you know it means no.

LUCIA: But why?

ROSINELLA: Massimo, talk to her.

MASSIMO: (*Shrugs*) Hello, Lucia.

ROSINELLA: Some help you! (*Tries gentle approach to Lucia*) Listen, hen, you're Italian, that makes you special. OK, so the Scotch people let their lassies go anywhere, do anything they like because they don't care as much. It's because I love you I want the best for you. You understand that, surely?

Lucia looks away, heard it all before.

ROSINELLA: (*Annoyed/to Massimo*) How come you always leave it to me? You tell her.

LUCIA: Please, Uncle Massimo?

MASSIMO: (*To Rosinella*) Why no just let her go?

Rosinella beginning to fly off the handle.

ROSINELLA: Oh, that's great! That's some help.

MASSIMO: You're too hard on her.

ROSINELLA: Oh aye, and you think you're that good. She's no to get going and that's that.

Lucia starts to cry.

LUCIA: You never let me go anywhere.

MASSIMO: See what you've done now.

ROSINELLA: That's right. Blame me. You want her mixing with all the toerags from the Auld Toon?

LUCIA: You never let me do anything.

ROSINELLA: Now come on, Lucia. You don't need to cry.

LUCIA: I just want to go to the wedding. One day. That's all I'm asking.

ROSINELLA: Now stop it, hen, come on. I'll make it up to you.

LUCIA: But WHY can't I go?

ROSINELLA: I've told you why no. Now come on, you can get anything you want.

LUCIA: (*Scoffs*) I NEVER get what I want. Never.

ROSINELLA: (*Shocked: to Massimo*) You hear that?

LUCIA: Not what 'I' want!

ROSINELLA: Please, Lucia, you know I hate to see you cry.

LUCIA: It's always got to be what YOU say. You never think about ME!

ROSINELLA: Now come on, Lucia, I said I'll make it up to you.

Massimo has been looking on: no help.

MASSIMO: You're being too soft with her.

ROSINELLA: Oh aye, you think you're that good. You talk to her.

Massimo prepares himself for the stern uncle bit, goes up to her.

MASSIMO: (*Very gently*) Lucia, please listen, hen ...

Lucia howls.

LUCIA: I wish I was back in Italy.

Her biggest gun: she storms off (to front shop).

Rosinella horrified.

ROSINELLA: Now look what you've done!

Rosinella about to run after her.

MASSIMO: Just leave her alone, Rosie, she'll calm down.

Rosinella stares at door to front shop, worried, something dawning on her.

ROSINELLA: Did you see the state she was in?

MASSIMO: I don't see why you don't just let her go to the wedding. She'll enjoy it. You go with her, keep an eye on her. I'll manage.

ROSINELLA: It's not the wedding that's worrying me, Massimo.

MASSIMO: Then what?

ROSINELLA: You don't see it, do you? It's up to me to see everything.

MASSIMO: See what?

ROSINELLA: Why do you think she was in that state, eh?

MASSIMO: Over the wedding.

ROSINELLA: Stupid eejit. Over Hughie, you mean.

MASSIMO: Hughie?

ROSINELLA: You no see the way he looks at our Lucia? He's crazy for her.

MASSIMO: Away you go. They grew up together.

ROSINELLA: She's to marry an Italian.

MASSIMO: For God's sake, Rosie, she's no asking to marry him, just to go to his brother's wedding. You worry too much.

ROSINELLA: No, Massimo. I don't worry enough. It's been going on before my eyes and I've never seen it till tonight.

MASSIMO: Seen what?

ROSINELLA: It's bad enough he's fell for her. But don't tell me she's to get falling for him. I'll soon put a stop to this before it starts.

MASSIMO: (*Groans*) Rosie ...

ROSINELLA: Italians are not interested in a lassie that's been out with anybody else – especially the Scotch men. They like a girl that's kept herself for them. I'm surprised at you.

MASSIMO: What have I done now?

ROSINELLA: Are you forgetting what this country did to the Italians during the war? (*Massimo groans*) They took you out of here as if you were a thief.

MASSIMO: Listen, Rosie, all I care about the war is that it's over. I lost ma faither, ma brother and four years out ma life.

ROSINELLA: Well, I'll never get over it.

MASSIMO: Neither will I. But everybody suffered. Not just us.

ROSINELLA: Italians have got to stick together.

MASSIMO: Then come to Italy with me, Rosie, what do you say?

Rosinella uncomfortable at mention of Italy.

ROSINELLA: No ... I don't think so.

MASSIMO: A wee holiday. The three of us.

ROSINELLA: Not yet, Massimo. You go, yourself. I don't mind.

MASSIMO: Everybody was asking for you when I was over. Asking why you've never been back. Please, Rosie, I'm dying to show you my daddy's house. You can help me make it nice. Next year, maybe, eh? How about it, Rosie?

ROSINELLA: I'm not going anywhere, Massimo, not until I see Lucia settled. (*A beat*) You think she's calmed down now? I think I'll take her to Glasgow on Saturday, go round the shops, get her something nice, take her to Palombo's to get her hair done. I'll go and tell her.

Scene Three

Hughie's house: Later that night

Hughie and Bridget.

Hughie, holding his jacket, rummaging in pocket.

HUGHIE: I nearly forgot. Where is it?

BRIDGET: What's this?

HUGHIE: It's money for Davie and Charmaine.

BRIDGET: (*Interested/pleased*) Really? Who from?

HUGHIE: Mrs Pedreschi.

BRIDGET: (*Scoffs*) Does she want a receipt for it?

HUGHIE: Ha ha! Well, I think it was very nice of her.

BRIDGET: So does she, I bet you. Is my mammy sleeping?

HUGHIE: Aye.

BRIDGET: I'm dead beat, so I am. I'll be glad when
    Saturday's by with. Oh here, you know Charmaine's
    sister, Yvonne – she's the chief bridesmaid? She was
    asking for you tonight, asking if you were bringing
    someone to the wedding. Three or four times she
    must've asked me.

HUGHIE: I hope you said I was.

BRIDGET: Why? Are you?

HUGHIE: I just don't want HER hanging around me.

BRIDGET: But you have asked someone?

HUGHIE: Well, yes, I have ASKED someone. But I don't
  know if she's coming yet.

BRIDGET: Anyone I know? (*Sees the hopeless look in his eye*) Oh
  Hughie, not Lucia Pedreschi?

HUGHIE: Ianelli actually. And so what if I've asked her?

BRIDGET: You surely know yourself she'll no come. Even if
  she wants to –

HUGHIE: (*Interrupting*) She does.

BRIDGET: (*Carrying on*) ... Even if she wants to, she'd never
  get allowed. That's Mrs Pedreschi for you! Oh aye, she
  can shove money in a poke and think she's doing you
  a good turn. I can just hear her – 'Just give that to your
  brother' – and all the time she's looking down her nose
  at you. Typical 'eye-ties'.

HUGHIE: I'll not hear a word against the Pedreschis, Bridget.
  They've treated me like one of the family.

BRIDGET: And that's where it will end, son, because you're
  not. They'll TREAT you like one of the family, so long as
  you don't start thinking like one, or acting like one.

Hughie depressed: Bridget sympathetic.

BRIDGET: Cheer up, Hughie. You're young, there's more to life than working in a shop every night.

HUGHIE: I like working there.

BRIDGET: You should be out enjoying yourself.

HUGHIE: I'm alright the way I am.

BRIDGET: You should be going to the dancing, get yourself a girlfriend.

HUGHIE: I'm not bothered.

BRIDGET: You know, I could shake you at times. You're going to let life pass you by.

HUGHIE: It's my life, Bridget.

BRIDGET: I just don't want you to end up like me.

HUGHIE: What? You mean a bus conductress?

BRIDGET: Very funny. What I meant was –

HUGHIE: – on the shelf.

BRIDGET: Well, I might've phrased it differently myself.

HUGHIE: Anyway, she might get coming.

BRIDGET: Even if she did, Hughie, nothing can come of it. Forget her.

HUGHIE: I don't want to.

She holds out her arms.

BRIDGET: Come on, Tweedledum.

HUGHIE: What?

BRIDGET: Might as well get in some dancing practice. Looks like we're going to be stuck with each other.

Hughie smiles and they waltz off stage.

Scene Four

Following Saturday: Street (Glasgow)

Lucia and Rosinella in: carrying parcels: they stop: Rosinella holds on to Lucia, takes foot out of shoe and rubs it: Lucia huffy.

ROSINELLA: Oh my feet are killing me.

LUCIA: I really wish you wouldn't try to bargain with the shop assistants, Auntie Rosinella. Nobody else does it.

ROSINELLA: But it's alright for me. I'm Italian.

LUCIA: It's SO embarrassing.

ROSINELLA: Your hair's lovely.

LUCIA: I prefer the way I do it myself, actually. (*She looks at her watch*)

ROSINELLA: Well I think they did it just lovely – and they were that pleased to see you.

Lucia looks at her watch, sighs.

LUCIA: They'll be sitting down to the meal, now.

ROSINELLA: Who? The Palombos?

LUCIA: No. At the wedding.

Rosinella shakes her head in disgust, gathers some parcels and goes.

Lucia is left, a few parcels at her feet.

Bring up music of 'Gay Gordons', Bridget and Hughie in, dutifully
    doing the dance: they do a couple of turns, then take confetti out
    and throw it: waving and shouting 'Goodbye' and 'All the best', etc.
    Their waves and shouts die down, they're left alone: while Bridget
    and Hughie talk, Lucia starts to twiddle the charms on her bracelet.

BRIDGET: So, she didn't come?

HUGHIE: No.

BRIDGET: You didn't expect her to, did you?

HUGHIE: I suppose not.

BRIDGET: Listen, son, I wish you'd get another job. Give
    yourself a chance to forget her.

HUGHIE: I don't want to.

BRIDGET: You'd have no problem finding a girlfriend – if
    you'd just push yourself a bit – a bit more 'oomph'.

HUGHIE: I'm no interested in anybody else.

BRIDGET: You like her that much?

HUGHIE: (*Nods*) I suppose I do.

BRIDGET: But – what if she's out of reach?

HUGHIE: I still don't want anybody else.

BRIDGET: Think what you're saying, Hughie. Would you
    really want to go through life, loving the one person you
    can't have, rather than looking for someone that might
    make you happy?

HUGHIE: Aye, I would. I know it sounds daft but I would. And I don't expect you to understand.

BRIDGET: But I do understand, son. (*A beat*) I mean, I can IMAGINE what that must be like.

HUGHIE: So don't tell me to forget her.

BRIDGET: So what you going to do about it?

HUGHIE: I don't know.

BRIDGET: Have you told her how you feel?

HUGHIE: No exactly, no.

BRIDGET: Why not? You just going to worship from afar?

HUGHIE: No.

BRIDGET: Then why haven't you told her?

HUGHIE: (*Struggling for an answer*) I don't know really ... I suppose I never really ... Och, it's no so easy ...

BRIDGET: Put it this way. If you love someone, then maybe you ought to tell them. There might come a time when you look back and wish you had.

HUGHIE: I'd like to but ...

BRIDGET: And don't you think, if someone is loved, they have the right to know? Think how precious that could be to someone. The difference it could make to their choices in life.

HUGHIE: What will I do, Bridget?

BRIDGET: Tell her.

HUGHIE: Tell her what?

BRIDGET: Tell her – you love her?

HUGHIE: Just go up to her and –

BRIDGET: – tell her.

HUGHIE: Right, I will.

BRIDGET: Now.

HUGHIE: Now?

BRIDGET: Yes – now. Don't leave it too late.

Lights down on Bridget, up on Lucia: Bridget crouches and starts to pick up confetti: Hughie approaches Lucia, with determination.

HUGHIE: Lucia, I –

LUCIA: (*Interrupting, holding out her arm to show off bracelet*) Do you like my new charm?

HUGHIE: It's … it's lovely, I really like it. It's really a nice one. (*A beat*) What is it?

LUCIA: It's an oyster. Look – look closely – there's the wee pearl inside. See?

HUGHIE: Lucia, I –

LUCIA: And there's my wee Cinderella coach. Sweet isn't it? And look at this one. It looks like a shoe, but you open it up and there's the old woman with all her children. See?

HUGHIE: Lucia, there's something I want to –

LUCIA: Have you seen this one? It's a real pound note, all folded up neatly in a wee glass box.

HUGHIE: Lucia – I –

LUCIA: And look at this one. It spins. You flick it round and look closely you'll see it says –

HUGHIE: I love you.

Lucia laughs.

LUCIA: No – 'Happy Birthday' – look again ...

Hughie's nerve has gone: he backs off, Lucia carries on fiddling with her bracelet: Hughie up to Bridget.

BRIDGET: Well? (*Sees his face*) You didn't tell her?

HUGHIE: (*Defensive*) It's not that easy.

BRIDGET: I know it's not. Come here. Why don't you write to her? (*He pulls back*) No, listen. Write her a letter, tell her how you feel. A letter is something that can be cherished. She can read it again and again. She can get to know it off by heart, keep it safe for the rest of her life.

Scene Five

Pedreschi's shop: A week or so later

Hughie on his own.

Lucia in.

LUCIA: Hello, Hughie.

Hughie looks up: delighted.

HUGHIE: Lucia! I never saw you come in. You staying long?

LUCIA: No, I'm just passing. I came in to get some money for the shopping.

HUGHIE: I bet you're going to buy something nice to wear.

LUCIA: I wish I was. I've to get something for tonight's dinner.

HUGHIE: You?

LUCIA: I know. Don't laugh. I'm doing the cooking these days. Auntie Rosinella says I've to learn to look after the house. Don't ask me why.

HUGHIE: Do you like it?

LUCIA: I hate it.

HUGHIE: Lucia?

LUCIA: Hughie?

HUGHIE: Lucia?

LUCIA: Hughie?

HUGHIE: I wish you wouldn't do that –

LUCIA: I'm sorry. What is it?

Hughie goes to his jacket: takes out an envelope: gives it to her.

LUCIA: What's this?

HUGHIE: Just a letter. I've had it for a few days – I wasn't
   sure when I'd see you.

She goes to open it. He stops her.

HUGHIE: Not here.

Lucia looks searchingly at him.

Rosinella in: Lucia pockets the letter hastily.

Rosinella annoyed when she sees the two of them together.

ROSINELLA: What you doing here, Lucia?

LUCIA: I came to get some money.

ROSINELLA: You finished those potatoes yet, Hughie?

HUGHIE: Aye.

ROSINELLA: Then go and set the tables.

HUGHIE: I've done that.

ROSINELLA: Then go and find something else to do.

Hughie hovers, looks at Lucia, then goes.

ROSINELLA: I left money on the sideboard for the shopping.

LUCIA: I'm sick fed up stuck in that house. Why don't YOU go home and I'll work here?

ROSINELLA: Where is it?

LUCIA: Where's what?

ROSINELLA: Give me it.

LUCIA: What?

ROSINELLA: Fine you know. The letter.

LUCIA: What letter?

ROSINELLA: The letter he gave you. Now come on, I saw you hide it.

LUCIA: I never.

ROSINELLA: Give it to me.

Rosinella reaches out for Lucia's pocket, Lucia pulls back and takes it out herself and gives it to her. Hughie in background. Has looked in, but is not seen: he slips away.

ROSINELLA: What's this, eh? He's writing to you now, eh?

Rosinella opens it, takes it out.

ROSINELLA: I knew it. It's a letter.

She looks at it: frustrated because she can't read: thrusts it back at Lucia.

ROSINELLA: What's it say?

LUCIA: I don't know – it doesn't matter. I'll just chuck it.

ROSINELLA: I want to know what it says. Read it for me.

LUCIA: Auntie Rosinella, I don't know what's wrong with you these days.

ROSINELLA: Just read it.

Lucia starts to read letter: she has to think on her feet.

LUCIA: It's just ... just a letter.

ROSINELLA: What's it say?

LUCIA: It just says ... it just says ... Have I heard the new Guy Mitchell ... ? It's really good ... he says ... and eh ... Would I ask my Uncle Massimo to get it for the juke box ... ? Because he thinks it would be good ... for the customers ... So he does ... and so do I ... as well ... I think so too.

ROSINELLA: I don't believe you.

LUCIA: No, it is good. You not heard it? (*Sings/tries to cajole*) 'I never felt more like singing the blues, 'cause I never thought that I'd ever lose your love, dear. You got me singing the blues. I never felt more like ...'

ROSINELLA: Give me that. (*Grabs letter*)

LUCIA: (*Pleading*) Auntie Rosinella.

ROSINELLA: Don't you 'Auntie Rosinella' me. I didn't want to have to do this but you're making me. I want you to stay away from that Hughie Devlin, you hear?

LUCIA: But why?

ROSINELLA: I don't want you seeing him.

LUCIA: Hughie's my pal.

ROSINELLA: I don't want you talking to him.

LUCIA: I don't understand.

ROSINELLA: Just stay away.

LUCIA: I won't. You can't make me.

ROSINELLA: Alright then, lady, I'll fix you. I'll get rid of him.

LUCIA: (*Shocked*) You wouldn't.

ROSINELLA: I would in a minute. Jumped up wee piece of nothing thinks because he works here he can look at you. Him?

LUCIA: You'd do that to Hughie?

ROSINELLA: And you'd thank me for it one day. You think I brought you up to throw yourself away on the likes of him?

LUCIA: I can't believe you're saying this. (*A beat*) You've changed, Auntie Rosinella.

ROSINELLA: I've just opened my eyes, that's all.

LUCIA: I'm going to speak to my Uncle Massimo.

ROSINELLA: No you're not, lady. You're going home. I'm going to speak to your Uncle Massimo. I'm going to show him this. He'll sort you out.

Lucia goes.

Rosinella stands silently fuming with letter: lights up on Massimo, looking worried: they approach each other, each with a letter in hand: Rosinella in righteous determination, Massimo in trepidation: they speak simultaneously.

ROSINELLA:	MASSIMO:
Massimo, I want to speak to you.	Can I have a wee word, Rosie?

Rosinella launches in.

ROSINELLA: Massimo, this has gone far enough. You can't keep saying I'm imagining it. You need to do something instead of leaving it all to me.

MASSIMO: After you, Rosie.

ROSINELLA: I want you to read this, tell me what it says.

MASSIMO: What's that?

ROSINELLA: This letter.

MASSIMO: What letter?

ROSINELLA: This letter to Lucia. A letter!

MASSIMO: (*Interested/takes it*) Who from?

ROSINELLA: Hughie. And what's more, she's told me a lie. I caught him giving it to her and she tried to hide it. What you waiting for? Tell me what it says.

MASSIMO: No, Rosie, you don't read other people's letters. It's no right.

ROSINELLA: Oh and you think you're that good. This is SERIOUS, Massimo. You don't see it, you don't WANT to see it, but if we don't do something now – and I don't care what it is – that lassie could end up with Hughie Devlin.

MASSIMO: It doesn't matter, Rosie.

ROSINELLA: How can you say it doesn't matter? I've brought her up since my sister died and I've loved her enough for two mammies.

MASSIMO: I mean it doesn't matter now, Rosie. It's out of our hands.

ROSINELLA: What you saying? You're saying it's too late? They've fell for each other and that's that? Forget it?

MASSIMO: No, Rosie, if you'd just calm down and let me speak. This is serious.

ROSINELLA: (*Mock jubilation*) I don't believe it. At last he's taken me serious. He's listening.

Massimo holds Rosinella firmly by her two arms.

MASSIMO: Rosie, I've had a letter from Luigi. He's sent for Lucia. She's to go home.

Silence: Rosinella horror-struck/in disbelief: Massimo keeps hold of her, she stares at him.

ROSINELLA: For a holiday?

MASSIMO: To live.

ROSINELLA: (*Mutters*) No ... no ... no ... you're wrong ... You're wrong ...

MASSIMO: Rosie ...

ROSINELLA: He can't ... he can't do that to me ... He can't do that ...

MASSIMO: (*Looks at letter*) He says he can never repay us for all our kindness in looking after –

ROSINELLA: (*Interrupting/grabs letter*) Give me that.

She scans letter but of course can't read it. Massimo continues without it.

MASSIMO: – all our kindness in looking after Lucia for
　　him –

ROSINELLA: (*Angry*) 'Looking after?' – we brought her up.
　　And I didn't do it for him. You tell him that. I did it for
　　my sister.

MASSIMO: – he says he never wanted to be separated from
　　her all these years, but what with the war –

ROSINELLA: Just what can HE give her? What, eh?

MASSIMO: – says he wants her to be with her brothers, who
　　are all longing to meet her.

ROSINELLA: (*Scoffs*) He's got five sons and four walls. Hasn't
　　even got a wall for each son!

MASSIMO: (*Gently admonishing*) Rosinella!

ROSINELLA: How can he do this?

MASSIMO: Rosie, please.

ROSINELLA: He thinks he can do this? He's daft. He must
　　be daft.

MASSIMO: Rosie, will you listen, please? You remember
　　the night before we brought Lucia back. We sat up.
　　Remember? We said we were frightened for just one
　　thing. Loving a child that's not your own is the hardest
　　love of all. The more you love them, the more pain you
　　get when they have to go back.

ROSINELLA: (*In disbelief*) That's nineteen years ago.

MASSIMO: I know. But we agreed then that we would be strong when it happened to us. We said we would be ready for it.

ROSINELLA: What? And you're ready for this, are you?

Massimo shakes his head, distraught.

MASSIMO: God, no.

ROSINELLA: Then stop being so bloody stupid.

Scene Six

Ginger store

Hughie in, sits down, despondent mood: opens bottle of ginger (maybe takes bottle out of his overall pocket) and slugs: belches: wipes his mouth with his sleeve, takes another slug.

LUCIA: God, Hughie Devlin, you've not changed, have you?

He nearly chokes: Lucia gets up from behind boxes.

HUGHIE: Lucia! What are you doing here?

LUCIA: I come here to think.

HUGHIE: So do I.

She comes out from behind boxes, also clutching bottle of ginger (maybe his is orange and hers is cola): they sit side by side, drinking.

LUCIA: Saluti!

HUGHIE: Cheers. Lucia?

LUCIA: Hughie?

HUGHIE: Lucia?

LUCIA: Hughie?

HUGHIE: I wish you wouldn't do that.

LUCIA: Sorry. What was it?

HUGHIE: No, nothing. (*A beat*) So, you're off on Sunday, are you?

LUCIA: Uh-huh.

HUGHIE: Lucky you.

LUCIA: Can I tell you something?

HUGHIE: Aye.

LUCIA: I'm scared.

HUGHIE: What? Of flying?

LUCIA: No. Just scared. I want to go and I don't want to go. Does that makes sense?

HUGHIE: Yes.

LUCIA: I want to see my daddy but I don't even remember what he looks like.

HUGHIE: If it was my daddy I would want to see him.

LUCIA: And I'll have brothers and cousins. Same as you've got.

HUGHIE: That's right. You'll like that. (*Pause*) Do you – think you'll ever come back – to stay – one day – ever?

LUCIA: Hughie, about your letter –

HUGHIE: (*Interrupting*) It's alright. I know what happened.

LUCIA: You do?

HUGHIE: I saw your Auntie Rosinella take it off you. I'm
  sorry if it got you into any trouble.

LUCIA: No, she never read it.

HUGHIE: But she got it before you did?

LUCIA: (*Hesitates*) Yes. (*A beat*) What was in the letter, Hughie?

HUGHIE: Oh ... nothing.

LUCIA: Nothing?

HUGHIE: Nothing important. Just ... Oh, I can't even
  remember now.

LUCIA: Will you write to me in Italy?

HUGHIE: Do you want me to?

LUCIA: Only if you want to.

Pause.

HUGHIE: Lucia, there's something I have to tell you.

Lucia takes bottle from her lips, wipes mouth, looks up at him expectantly.

LUCIA: Yes, Hughie?

HUGHIE: Lucia?

LUCIA: Yes, Hughie?

HUGHIE: Lucia – (*He takes a deep breath*) – Lucia – (*loses nerve*) You're drinking my ginger.

He swops bottles back: Lucia sighs.

LUCIA: Oh, Hughie. (*A beat*) I thought I was your ginger-sister.

HUGHIE: God, that's right. You were my ginger-sister – ARE my ginger-sister. It was supposed to be for ever.

LUCIA: That's right. And you're my ginger-brother.

Hughie's cue to say he loves her: he hovers: misses it.

HUGHIE: I can't believe you're going away.

LUCIA: (*Prompting*) Hughie – about that letter?

HUGHIE: Just go off and forget about it, eh?

LUCIA: I don't want to.

HUGHIE: Please, Lucia.

LUCIA: Why?

HUGHIE: It's not important.

LUCIA: It might have been to me.

HUGHIE: Do you want me to write to you in Italy?

LUCIA: Not if it's not important, I don't.

HUGHIE: I didn't say it wasn't important.

LUCIA: Not in so many words.

HUGHIE: I said it ISN'T important.

LUCIA: Oh excuse me!

HUGHIE: Look. What was in the letter WAS important, at the time, probably. But it is not important any more because you are going away to start a new life.

LUCIA: And what WAS in it – at the time?

HUGHIE: I forget.

LUCIA: But it WAS important – probably?

HUGHIE: Aye.

LUCIA: But you said you forget.

HUGHIE: I do.

LUCIA: So how do you know it was important?

HUGHIE: Well, it must've been, mustn't it? Otherwise I wouldn't have wrote it.

LUCIA: No point in writing to me in Italy then, is there?

HUGHIE: Why not?

LUCIA: Well, it takes about three weeks to get there. By the time I read it, you'll forget what's in it.

HUGHIE: Do you no want me to write then?

LUCIA: I didn't say that.

HUGHIE: So you do want me to write?

LUCIA: Not if it's not important enough for you to even remember what's in it.

Hughie totally frustrated: goes to speak then stops and thinks.

HUGHIE: I don't like this game, Lucia.

LUCIA: And I don't like it either.

HUGHIE: Will I see you again before you go?

Lucia about to answer.

ROSINELLA: (*Voice from offstage: shouts*) Lucia. Lucia.

LUCIA: I better go.

She turns to go: Hughie puts his hand in his pocket, looks at something, thinks about it.

HUGHIE: Lucia – (*She stops*) It's my daddy's penknife. I want you to have it.

LUCIA: Hughie ... I ...

ROSINELLA: (*Voice from offstage: shouts*): Looooo – cheeeeee – aaaaaa.

HUGHIE: You better go.

Lucia looks at the knife in her hand, looks at Hughie, hugs him and goes.

Scene Seven

Rosinella rummaging frantically in big bin: cases in background.
Massimo in.

MASSIMO: What you doing, Rosie?

ROSINELLA: I just threw out a big pail of chips – and kept the peels. I can't even think straight any more.

Massimo pats her back.

MASSIMO: I know.

ROSINELLA: I took two baths this morning. I was up that early, I took one when I got up, then I forgot I'd had one and took another before I came out.

MASSIMO: Will you no change your mind and come to the airport?

ROSINELLA: (*Edgy*) You want to finish me altogether?

MASSIMO: You sure you'll be alright till I get back?

ROSINELLA: (*Annoyed*) Do I look alright?

Lucia in: coat on.

MASSIMO: Here she is. (*Awkward silence*) You sure you're alright for money, hen?

Lucia nods: she can't speak, does not know what to say.

MASSIMO: Right. I'll take your cases out to the car.

He goes: Rosinella has to steel herself to look at her but manages to be strong.

LUCIA: Auntie Rosinella.

ROSINELLA: You look lovely, hen. Listen, Lucia, there's a home for you here. I never want you to forget that. OK?

Lucia nods.

ROSINELLA: You've to want for nothing, OK?

Lucia nods.

ROSINELLA: And when your daddy sees you, sees the fine lady I brought you up to be, as God is my judge standing here, he'll send you back to me.

Lucia throws her arms round Rosinella's neck and kisses her and hurries out.

Rosinella is left – empty: she looks round, not knowing what to do with herself: she goes in to front shop.

Hughie in, at a run.

HUGHIE: Lucia!

He looks around: it is empty: he turns away sadly: he stays on stage.

Scene Eight

Back shop: Two weeks later

Massimo humming 'Santa Lucia'.

Massimo in from front shop with tray of fish: he starts to batter them (or something). Hughie also working nearby.

Massimo's humming gets louder, he starts to bring in the words 'Santa Lucia'. On the 'Lucia' Rosinella appears from the front shop and silences him with a look.

MASSIMO: Cheer up, Rosie, for God's sake.

ROSINELLA: Maybe I don't want to cheer up. You thought of that, eh?

Hughie turns to her.

HUGHIE: Any word from Lucia, Mrs Pedreschi?

ROSINELLA: Not since you asked me yesterday, there's no. Not that it's any business of yours.

Hughie, embarrassed, goes out.

MASSIMO: (*Annoyed*) That was uncalled for.

ROSINELLA: It's time you got rid of him.

MASSIMO: Hughie?

ROSINELLA: Who does he think he is, asking for news of Lucia as if he were one of the family?

MASSIMO: For God's sake, Rosie. They grew up together.

ROSINELLA: I want you to get rid of him.

MASSIMO: What harm has he done to you?

ROSINELLA: He reminds me too much of Lucia. How will I ever get over her with him around? I want him out of here.

Massimo looks at her long and hard. Realises she is serious.

MASSIMO: Maybe it's time I had a word with him, right enough.

He lifts up his tray of fish and goes: Rosinella carries on working.

Bridget in, stands watching her for a bit.

BRIDGET: Mrs Pedreschi.

Rosinella looks up, surprised to see Bridget, takes a moment to register.

ROSINELLA: Well, well. Bridget Devlin. I don't think I've seen you since ... sit down.

BRIDGET: I'm alright.

Bridget's stance is disconcerting Rosinella.

ROSINELLA: Is there something wrong? (*A beat*) It's no your mother, is it?

BRIDGET: It's no my mother, no.

ROSINELLA: How is she?

BRIDGET: Good days and bad days. Thinks my da got killed in the war. Still, I don't suppose it matters, really. Just another old Scotch woman.

ROSINELLA: What is it you want, Bridget? If it's Hughie you're looking for, he's outside.

BRIDGET: Good. I don't want him to hear this.

ROSINELLA: Hear what? Tell me what you want.

BRIDGET: I knew you'd try to split them up. I warned our Hughie, but I never knew the lengths you'd go to.

ROSINELLA: What you talking about?

BRIDGET: You sent her back, didn't you? Didn't care who gets hurt. After all these years you sent her away.

ROSINELLA: Who?

BRIDGET: Lucia. Who else?

ROSINELLA: Send Lucia away? Me?

BRIDGET: Well, you did it to me, but you're no getting doing it to my brother.

ROSINELLA: I don't want to hear any more. What did I ever do to you?

BRIDGET: What did you do to me? You told me Franco
    didn't love me. You made me believe I was nothing
    to him – just a wee Scottish tart for him to
    practise on.

ROSINELLA: In God's name, Bridget, that's all in the past.

BRIDGET: To you maybe. But there's no a day goes past that
    it's no with me. Franco loved me. Franco loved me.

ROSINELLA: Franco's dead – and may God forgive you, lady,
    for dragging his name through the mud.

*This remark knocks Bridget off her guard and Rosinella gathers her
strength.*

ROSINELLA: Now, I didn't want this fight with you, and
    I don't have to explain nothing to you. But just you
    hear this. I didn't send Lucia away, I could just as
    easily tear out my own heart. But I'm no sorry she's
    away from your brother. I cannie deny it. No harm
    to the boy. I've nothing against him. OK? Now that's
    it finished. We'll forget this conversation ever took
    place.

BRIDGET: As easy as that.

ROSINELLA: Yes.

BRIDGET: All forgotten.

ROSINELLA: I'll never mention it again.

BRIDGET: If you knew the damage you've caused.

ROSINELLA: (*Angry*) That's it. I've had enough. I don't have to stand here and listen to this. You think I'm not suffering? Lucia's more than a niece to me, more than somebody else's lassie that I brought up and grew to love. She's like the child I could never have.

Silence: Bridget thinks, then decides.

BRIDGET: The child you never had, eh, Mrs Pedreschi? What about the child I never had?

ROSINELLA: (*Dismissive*) What you going on about now?

BRIDGET: Do you remember that night, I came to see you? I was pregnant.

Rosinella shakes her head.

ROSINELLA: What you saying?

BRIDGET: I was pregnant and it was Franco's baby.

Rosinella backs off in disbelief.

BRIDGET: Franco's baby. I was desperate. I didn't know where to turn. I'd just lost my da and my mammy was leaning on me. It was what you told me that night that made me decide. What else could I have done?

Slow realisation with Rosinella, increasing horror as Bridget speaks.

It cost me two pound. I went round at seven and was out at quarter to eight. The woman who did it was really nice. You must know her, she probably comes into the shop. 'Come in,' she said, 'come away in.' She took my coat and left it by the fire. She gave me a brandy and told me to lie on the table. Told me not to worry, she was very good. Liked helping people, she said. I heard water being poured and a clinky sound like metal on glass. She warmed her hands before she started, to make me comfortable, she said, and she spoke the whole time, a nice, easy voice to listen to ...

When it was over we had a cup of tea and a chat. She told me I should rest but that would be easy. Now that it was behind me I could sleep like a baby. If anything were to go wrong – which it never did with her girls, but just in case – I was no to come back and no to tell anyone where it was done. Then she helped me into my coat which was all warm and cosy and I left. When I got out I went into my pockets for my gloves. I couldn't find them so I went back in. She jumped up when she saw me. She was throwing something on the fire ... You see, I thought Franco didn't love me. You told me that. And I believed you. That's the reason I did what I did that night. But I've never told another living soul, Mrs Pedreschi, not until now.

Rosinella now on her knees, blesses herself: lights down on her, but she stays there: lights up on Hughie and Massimo in ginger store.

They are in mid-discussion.

MASSIMO: I'm to blame as well.

HUGHIE: No you're not, Mr Pedreschi.

MASSIMO: Yes I am, son. I should have realised what was going on. You two kids are crazy about each other. Why did you not talk to me before?

HUGHIE: What for? I've nothing to offer Lucia. I'm no an Italian – I've no money, no prospects, I've no even got a decent jo– (*Stops short*) Sorry, Mr Pedreschi.

MASSIMO: I've been thinking, son – now I'm no just saying this – I've been thinking of getting an ice cream van. I've been meaning to talk to you about it. I want you to learn to drive – I'll pay for your lessons – and we'll get you a run. You'll make money – I'll make money. What do you think, eh?

HUGHIE: It's awful good of you, Mr Pedreschi, but ... I ... can't work here any more.

MASSIMO: You're kidding?

HUGHIE: I'll not see you stuck. I'll stay till you find someone else.

MASSIMO: Hughie – son – you've worked here since you were a wean.

HUGHIE: I know, Mr Pedreschi, and I've always enjoyed it.

MASSIMO: Then change your mind. Come on, son.

HUGHIE: I'm sorry.

MASSIMO: I don't want to lose you, son.

HUGHIE: I've got to leave.

MASSIMO: First Lucia, now you. I've had the pair of you round about my feet for the past fifteen years. We must be able to work out something, son. Come on.

HUGHIE: You've been good to me, Mr Pedreschi. It's got nothing to do with you.

MASSIMO: Then who has it to do with? (*A beat: realisation: he looks in direction of Rosinella*) … No don't tell me, I think I know.

Lights down on Hughie, up on Rosinella.

Bridget gone now. Rosinella seated, head in hands: looks up wearily when Massimo approaches.

Massimo looking at her very coldly: no sympathy at all.

MASSIMO: It's time we talked about Hughie –

ROSINELLA: (*Interrupting*) Take me to Italy, Massimo.

MASSIMO: What?

ROSINELLA: I want to go to Italy.

MASSIMO: Why – all of a sudden?

ROSINELLA: Just to get away from here.

MASSIMO: But why now?

ROSINELLA: Because I can't face it here. There's too much heartache.

MASSIMO: How long for?

ROSINELLA: I don't care.

MASSIMO: What about the shop?

ROSINELLA: Do what you like with it. Shut it. Sell it. I don't care if we never come back.

Massimo looks at her in disbelief.

MASSIMO: You mean that, don't you?

ROSINELLA: I just want away.

MASSIMO: When I think of the times I've asked you to come to Italy with me. Oh, but you always had an excuse ready. Now – because YOU'RE unhappy, because YOU miss Lucia – we've just to go. Just like that. To hell with the shop, to hell with everything I've worked for. To hell with everything except what YOU want.

ROSINELLA: If you knew what I've been through.

MASSIMO: Oh Rosie, Rosie, do you think I don't know? 'What you've been through.' It's all I've ever heard. But what about the rest of us? Do we no go through anything? What about Lucia – what about Hughie – what about me?

ROSINELLA: Massimo ... please. Don't do this to me.

MASSIMO: But you really don't care for anyone else's pain except your own, do you? I never realised that before and I wish to God I didn't now. All these years, I've known what it meant to you, no being able to have a family. God knows, you never tried to hide it. Never. But did you ever once think what it's been like for me? Did you ever think maybe I would have liked a child? A son to work alongside me, to plan things with. A son to leave my shop to ... (*Voice breaks*) But you! You never think of anyone but yourself.

ROSINELLA: Lucia. I want Lucia.

MASSIMO: (*With contempt*) Oh aye, 'Lucia, Lucia'. You love her that much you don't want her to love anyone else. You love her that much, nobody else has to get loving her. Oh aye, you love Lucia alright.

He goes: Rosinella shattered: Hughie in, she doesn't see him at first. She turns and looks at him, very sadly.

ROSINELLA: Hughie ...

HUGHIE: Mrs Pedreschi.

ROSINELLA: Hughie, son – I'm sorry.

She starts to cry: he does not know what to do. She reaches her hand out to him and he puts his arm round her and she cries.

Scene Nine

Italy: Outdoors/around Luigi's farm: Daytime

Lucia, weary look, carrying tub of dirty clothes, lets out a scream, drops the tub, dancing about with screaming ab-dabs, shouting (she's seen a creepy-crawly go up her arm).

LUCIA: (*Hysterics*) Get it off me. Get it off me. Oh mammy-daddy, mammy-daddy, get it off me, get it off me. Get it off me.

Luigi runs in, alarmed.

LUIGI: Che si passa?

LUCIA: Oh daddy, daddy, get it off me, get it off me.

She is jumping about so much he can't help her.

LUIGI: Ma che è?

LUCIA: A scorpion. A scorpion. A big black scorpion. It's in my hair, it's in my hair. Get it off me.

LUIGI: (*Firmly*) Fermati! Ma do' sta?

Lucia calms down: he rummages at the back of her neck, pulls something out in his two hands.

LUIGI: Eccolo.

LUCIA: (*Panics*) Don't let me see it. Don't let me see it.

LUIGI: Ma, fermati, Lucia. Non è uno scorpione. It's a
	spider – look!

*Shoves his cupped hands up to her face: she screams: he laughs –
	amused at her, not sadistic.*

LUCIA: I hate them. I hate them. I don't want to see them.

LUIGI: (*Puts an arm round her shoulder, affectionately*) Come
	here, you! Sei pazza. It's too long you've been away,
	eh? My wife, she thinks you're a lovely girl – 'Che
	bellezza', ha detto. Ma, she thinks you're lazy. Ho
	detto io, I says, 'She's no lazy. She's just no used to
	work. Ma, she'll learn.' È vero? Sì? È vero? Hmmmmm?
	Hmmmmm?

Lucia nods.

LUIGI: Brava! (*He tweaks her cheek with one hand, she smiles,
	trying to feel reassured. He holds up the other hand with the
	spider to her face*): Bzzzzz! Bzzzzzzzz!

She jumps: he laughs, ruffles her hair.

LUIGI: Got you that time, eh? Va bene, Lucia, when you're
	finished the clothes, you've to come up to the house. My
	wife's going to teach you to clean a chicken. OK?

*He drops the spider on the ground and crunches it with his foot: Lucia
	winces.*

LUCIA: You don't have to ... kill it. (*Too late*)

LUIGI: OK?

LUCIA: OK.

LUIGI: Today you work hard. Tomorrow's the feast day. La festa dell'Assunta. Ti piace?

Lucia nods.

LUIGI: Good girl. My Lucia. I'm going to help Michele set up the fireworks.

He tweaks her cheek and goes.

She starts to pick up the clothes she dropped.

Just before he goes offstage, Luigi turns and points.

LUIGI: (*Shouts*) Attenzione! A snake.

Lucia screams: he laughs, claps his hands and points at her: he goes.

Lucia kneels down, near to tears, picks up the clothes with her fingertips, shakes them, puts them in the tub: walks over to the wash-place – kneels down, picks up two stones and sets about trying to wash the clothes: she makes a real mess of it, gets more and more frustrated, ends up banging her fingers with one of the stones and throwing it away: she goes and picks it up and starts again.

Rosinella in, watches her for a moment: then up to her: very matter-of-fact.

ROSINELLA: Here. Let me do that.

LUCIA: Oh thanks, Auntie Rosinella.

ROSINELLA: Here's the way you do it. Now look. Just watch me. I used to do this when I was a wee girl.

LUCIA: Thanks, Auntie Rosinella, I just can't seem to get the hang ... (*It dawns on Lucia*) Auntie Rosinella! Oh, Auntie Rosinella. Oh, thank God it's you.

Lucia throws arms round her, almost knocks her over she hugs her so tight.

ROSINELLA: You pleased to see me, then?

LUCIA: Oh, Auntie Rosinella, what are you doing here?

ROSINELLA: Let me look at you.

Holds Lucia back, fixes her hair, tries to tidy her up a bit, dust her down, not really listening (maybe gets hanky out and spits on it and cleans Lucia's face a bit).

LUCIA: Oh, Auntie Rosinella, I've had to feed the pigs.

ROSINELLA: Is that right, hen?

LUCIA: And fetch the water ... and pick the olives.

ROSINELLA: Is that right?

LUCIA: And there's no bath.

ROSINELLA: Uh-huh.

LUCIA: And no lavvy pan.

ROSINELLA: Is that right?

LUCIA: And my shoes are all wasted. Look.

ROSINELLA: Right. You'll do.

LUCIA: What for?

ROSINELLA: Come on.

LUCIA: Oh, I get it. You're here for the feast aren't you?

ROSINELLA: What feast?

LUCIA: (*Thinks Rosinella's kidding*) What feast? The Feast of the Assumption.

ROSINELLA: Yes, that's right.

Starts to lead Lucia away.

LUCIA: Where are we going?

ROSINELLA: Your Uncle Massimo's.

Lucia looks at the washing.

LUCIA: What about ... ?

ROSINELLA: Leave that. It's alright. I've spoken to your daddy. He says you could come and help me clean the house.

They go.

Scene Ten

Massimo's house: Later that day

Lights up on Hughie, sweltering in the heat: puts jacket over back of a chair: shakes shirt to cool himself down a bit, particularly round the armpits: hears voices, hides: Rosinella and Lucia in: Rosinella breathless.

ROSINELLA: Mannaggia la miseria! What a climb. And this heat! Let me sit down.

Rosinella sits, Lucia looking around: sees jacket: her eyes light up.

LUCIA: (*Excited*) My Uncle Massimo's here too! Oh this is great.

ROSINELLA: And my feet are that sore –

LUCIA: Where is he?

ROSINELLA: I'll change into my flat shoes.

LUCIA: (*Shouts*) Uncle Massimo!

ROSINELLA: (*Wincing at the noise*) Lucia!

LUCIA: I can't wait to see him. (*Shouts*) Uncle Massimo!

ROSINELLA: He'll no can hear you, hen.

LUCIA: (*Shouts louder*) Uncle Massimo!

ROSINELLA: He's no there.

LUCIA: He can't be far. There's his jacket.

ROSINELLA: It's no his jacket.

LUCIA: Then whose – ?

Hughie out from hiding: Lucia stares in disbelief from Rosinella to Hughie and back again.

Rosinella gives her a reassuring nod: encouraging nod: Hughie holds out his arms and Lucia goes into them.

They are engrossed in their reunion, touching each other's faces, hands, delighting in each other.

Rosinella watches them: she turns away, a sad, faraway expression.

In background Lucia leaves Hughie sitting in sun: she comes up to Rosinella, throws her arms round her.

ROSINELLA: You happy?

LUCIA: Happy? I must be dreaming. I don't understand.

ROSINELLA: I think before you went we were all so heartbroken nobody could think straight. But we all got together and talked it all out. Me, your Uncle Massimo, Hughie, Bridget.

LUCIA: (*Surprised*) Bridget?

ROSINELLA: Who do you think's working in the shop?

LUCIA: (*More surprised*) Bridget?

ROSINELLA: She's really the one that's behind all this, you know.

LUCIA: (*Even more surprised*) Bridget?

ROSINELLA: You'll never know the half of it, Lucia.

LUCIA: So, Bridget's in the shop. Does that mean my Uncle Massimo's coming over?

ROSINELLA: No, hen, he's not.

LUCIA: Why not?

Rosinella shrugs, sadly.

ROSINELLA: We're no really getting on that well these days.

LUCIA: Don't tell me you've fallen out?

ROSINELLA: No, love, we're talking alright. I mean, you have to talk, don't you? But some things have been said between us, Lucia, and I ... I don't think he loves me any more.

LUCIA: Oh, Auntie Rosinella, of course he loves you.

Rosinella pulls herself together quickly, realising this is too heavy for Lucia.

ROSINELLA: You're right, my darling. What am I thinking of, eh? Now I'm going to have a wee lie down. You and Hughie have got a lot to talk about. And don't you worry about your daddy. Just you tell him I'll be up tonight to see him. We'll get it all sorted out.

Scene Eleven

Luigi's house: Later that evening

(The following is going on in the background, in silence)

Luigi sitting at a table.

*Lucia clears things from the table, gets a tablecloth and three glasses
and puts them on the table: Luigi does not lift a finger to help:
there might be an ashtray, or his glass, a foot away from him
and he gestures for Lucia to put it closer: when everything is at a
readiness he shoos her away, which will coincide with arrival of
Hughie and Rosinella.*

*While these preparations are going on, Hughie and Rosinella are
in the foreground, getting ready to go: Hughie, bare-chested,
sunburnt, Rosinella rubbing on calamine lotion.*

HUGHIE: Haaaaa! Waaaaa! Eeeeee! Ah! Oh! Oh! Oh! Oh! ...
(*Or words to that effect!*)

ROSINELLA: It's your own stupid fault. I told you to watch
the sun.

HUGHIE: I just wanted a tan.

ROSINELLA: You! You'll be lucky if you get freckles. (*Holds
out his shirt*) ... Here!

HUGHIE: Eeeee! Oh! Ah! Ah! ... (*It hurts as he puts it on*)

ROSINELLA: You ready? Let me look at you. (*He gets up. She
shakes her head*) You'll have to do. Come on. (*She nudges his
shoulder: he winces*)

They go: they pass Lucia leaving: they exchange looks, Lucia nods her head in the direction of her father's table: Rosinella squeezes her hand: Lucia pats Hughie's back and goes and kneels, outside, and waits: lights down on Lucia.

Rosinella and Hughie up to Luigi.

ROSINELLA: Buona sera.

LUIGI: Buona sera. Buona sera.

ROSINELLA: This is Hughie. Hughie Devlin.

LUIGI: (*Puzzled*) Come si chiama?

ROSINELLA: Hughie. Hughie. Hugh. Hugh ... Ugo. ('*Oo-go*')

LUIGI: Ah – Ugo. Va bene. (*Shakes his hand warmly, clasping his forearm: Hughie winces.*)

Luigi indicates chairs: lifts wine bottle.

LUIGI: Pigli una sedia. Vuoi qualcosa da bere?

HUGHIE: What did he say?

ROSINELLA: Just sit down and shut up.

LUIGI: (*Pointing to Hughie*) Questo parla italiano?

HUGHIE: What's he saying?

ROSINELLA: (*To Luigi*) No.

HUGHIE: No, what?

ROSINELLA: No, you don't speak Italian.

HUGHIE: (*Puzzled*) I know I don't.

ROSINELLA: (*To Hughie*) Just leave it to me.

They get seated with glasses of wine.

LUIGI: (*To Hughie*) Ti piace l'Italia?

ROSINELLA: (*Before Hughie gets words out*) He wants to know if you like Italy.

Hughie nods emphatically at Luigi, anxious to please.

HUGHIE: Oh yes. Yes. Very much. Very much. I really like it. Tell him I really like it. I like it a lot. I think it's ... fabulous.

LUIGI: È favolosa ... sì. Ho capito. (*Gestures upwards*) Fa attenzione al sole.

HUGHIE: What was that?

ROSINELLA: He says take care in the sun.

HUGHIE: (*To Luigi*) Right-oh! Yes. Thanks.

Silence: Luigi goes to top up Hughie's glass: Hughie puts his hand over it: Luigi insists/very genial/slaps him on back.

LUIGI: Ma beve. Bevi! Enjoy yourself, Ugo. Tomorrow's the feast-day. Bevi il vino. Accomodati. My house is your house. (*A beat/to Rosinella*) Who is he, anyway?

ROSINELLA: Works in the shop. A good worker, an awfy good worker. An awfy, awfy, awfy, awfy, awfy good worker, so he is. You want to hear Massimo about him. Thinks there's nobody like Hughie. Him and Lucia went to school together.

Hughie sits up at mention of their names.

HUGHIE: You're telling him about me and Lucia?

ROSINELLA: Yes.

HUGHIE: Right. Good. Tell him – tell him I love her with my heart and soul.

ROSINELLA: (*To Luigi*) I know he's no that much to look at.

HUGHIE: And tell him she loves me. Tell him she's always loved me.

ROSINELLA: (*To Luigi*) And I cannie tell you a lie – he hasn't got a penny to his name.

HUGHIE: And that we want to be together forever, our hearts united – like two lovebirds, up a tree in spring.

ROSINELLA: (*To Luigi*) And I know he's no very – (*Cuts off: to Hughie*) Where did you hear that?

HUGHIE: I don't know. It just came to me.

ROSINELLA: He's no had an easy time of it. Lost his daddy when he was just a wee boy.

LUIGI: (*To Hughie, filling his glass*) Bevi! (*Hughie resists/Luigi insists*)

HUGHIE: (*Thinks he's saying 'Cheers'*) Bevvy!

Luigi fills his own glass, eyes Hughie up and down.

LUIGI: (*To Rosinella*) I wouldn't have noticed if you hadn't said, but he is quite ugly, right enough.

ROSINELLA: (*Defensive*) He's no ugly. I wouldn't say he was ugly.

LUIGI: No. Maybe not. Maybe it's just the colour of his cheeks and his hair.

ROSINELLA: That's no his fault.

LUIGI: And he's not got much of a build, has he? He's kind of round-shouldered, isn't he?

ROSINELLA: (*Sharply to Hughie*) Sit up straight, you.

LUIGI: And what's that on his face?

Rosinella looks closely at Hughie.

ROSINELLA: He's peeling.

LUIGI: He's what? He got burnt in the sunshine? È pazzo, no? (*Leans over to Hughie, very emphatic, speaking very slowly*

*and deliberately to make him understand, accompanied by
exaggerated gestures – e.g. eyes squinting in the sun, wiping
away perspiration, pointing to sun in sky, sun beating down on
head, weariness, panting for breath, etc. Hughie trying to make
sense of it.)*

Fa – molto – caldo. Mol-to – cal-do. Trop-po – cal-do,
sì? Fa atttenzione al sole, eh? Troppo caldo, sì. Il sole.
Troppo caldo. Attenzione, eh?

HUGHIE: What's he saying?

ROSINELLA: (*In disbelief*) He says he keeps thinking it's
Wednesday.

LUIGI: (*To Hughie*) Va bene?

Hughie smiles at Luigi, shrugs at Rosinella.

HUGHIE: Have you no asked him yet?

ROSINELLA: I'm getting there. I'm getting there.

HUGHIE: Just ask, will you?

LUIGI: Allora! What was it you want to talk about? Lucia
says it's important, so I sent her away.

HUGHIE: (*To Luigi*) Lucia. Yes. (*To Rosinella*) Ask him.

ROSINELLA: So it is, Luigi. Hughie. Ugo. Well, he wants to
marry Lucia.

Luigi chokes on his wine.

ROSINELLA: And I'm no caring what he's got or no got. We'll see them alright. Me and Massimo. We've got a business over there. A good business. Nobody to leave it to.

Luigi still choking: Rosinella gets up and starts thumping his back.

ROSINELLA: What matters is these two young people love each other. And you don't need to worry about a thing. I'll pay for the wedding. I'll pay for everything. I'll even pay for you to come to Scozia to give her away ...

Luigi gets his breath and thumps fist on table.

LUIGI: Ma fermati! I'm not going to Scozia for any wedding.

ROSINELLA: They can get married here, then. It's all one to me. (*To Hughie*) Is that OK with you, Hughie son?

HUGHIE: What?

ROSINELLA: You don't mind getting married here?

HUGHIE: No, no at all.

ROSINELLA: Va bene, Luigi. That's alright with you? Will I call Lucia?

HUGHIE: (*To Luigi*) Lucia. Yes.

ROSINELLA: (*To Hughie*) Get her in.

LUIGI: (*Shouts*) Leave Lucia!

Rosinella puts a restraining hand on Hughie: he picks up the tension.

HUGHIE: Mrs Pedreschi ...?

LUIGI: (*Shouts*) She's not going to Scozia. She's not marrying any scozzese. She's staying here.

HUGHIE: Mrs Pedreschi ...?

Rosinella holds hand out to keep Hughie quiet.

ROSINELLA: (*Cajoling*) I know how you feel, Luigi, you've just got her back and you don't want to lose her again. But it'll be different this time – you got cut off because of the war. That's nobody's fault. They'll come and see you whenever they can. They'll bring your grandchildren to see you. You can come and visit them, bring your sons ...

HUGHIE: Mrs Pedreschi ...?

LUIGI: Will you stop making plans for Lucia? Lucia is MY lassie. I've got my own plans for Lucia.

HUGHIE: Mrs Pedreschi ...?

ROSINELLA: (*Beginning to lose the plot*) Porca miseria ... Luigi!

HUGHIE: Mrs Pedreschi ...?

LUIGI: I'm her daddy. She's my lassie.

ROSINELLA: I know fine well she's your lassie.

HUGHIE: Mrs Pedreschi ...?

ROSINELLA: I never says she wasn't your lassie.

HUGHIE: Mrs Pedreschi ...?

ROSINELLA: (*Screams at Hughie*) Will you stop calling me 'Mrs Pedreschi'?

HUGHIE: I ... what do you want me to call you?

ROSINELLA: (*Furious*) Anything. Anything but (*puts on namby-pamby voice*) 'Mrs Pedreschi. Mrs Pedreschi.' (*Pause, she quietens: realisation: turns to Luigi*) What plans?

Luigi smiles enigmatically, taps his nose.

ROSINELLA: You said you've got plans for Lucia.

LUIGI: She's my lassie.

ROSINELLA: What plans you got?

LUIGI: When the time comes for her to get married, you can still help if you want. Pay for this, pay for that – that's fine by me. I know how much she means to you. Va bene?

ROSINELLA: (*To Luigi*) What are you saying?

HUGHIE: Mrs Ped– (*Tentatively*) Auntie Rosinella?

ROSINELLA: (*To Luigi/annoyed*) You think I don't know your game. 'Your lassie, your lassie!' You brought her here to make her work, didn't you? I can see. I can see. It's all too much for your wife now, isn't it, eh? Five big boys, no one lassie and married onto a big lazy bastard like you. (*Rosinella regrets swearing the minute it's out.*)

HUGHIE: Auntie Rosinella ...?

ROSINELLA: Oh Dio, forget I said that. I shouldn't have said that.

HUGHIE: Auntie Rosinella ...?

LUIGI: Alright. Alright, I'll tell you.

ROSINELLA: I want to know.

LUIGI: I said I'll tell you.

HUGHIE: Auntie Rosinella ...

LUIGI: Lucia doesn't know yet, so don't you go saying to her.

HUGHIE: Auntie Rosinella?

ROSINELLA: (*To Hughie*) I'm not your bloody auntie.

HUGHIE: I just want ...

LUIGI: Lucia's engaged ... It's all arranged.

HUGHIE: What's going on ...?

ROSINELLA: (*Stunned: to Hughie*) She's engaged!

HUGHIE: Engaged! Who to?

ROSINELLA: No to you. (*To Luigi*) Who to?

LUIGI: Mario Santoni. Figlio di Angelo.

HUGHIE: Engaged?

ROSINELLA: (*To Luigi*) So, you've arranged it all, have you?

LUIGI: Me and Angelo shook hands on it, just last week.

ROSINELLA: Hughie. Hughie, do you hear that?

HUGHIE: What?

LUIGI: So you can tell the sunshine boy here, thank you very
    much but I'm sorry I have to say no.

HUGHIE: Hear what? How can she be engaged?

ROSINELLA: (*Backing off in disbelief*) There's something
    going on ... there's something I'm not seeing ...

HUGHIE: How can she be engaged?

ROSINELLA: (*To Hughie*) Will you wheesht! (*To Luigi*)
    Santoni? Santoni? Mario Santoni. Figlio di Angelo.
    Angelo? Angelo Santoni? (*Recognition/annoyed at herself
    for not seeing sooner*) Angelo Santoni! Of course. He's
    right ... next ... door ... to ... you. (*Only as she says this, the
    full realisation dawns*)

LUIGI: (*Nods*) Sì.

HUGHIE: See what?

ROSINELLA: He's got the best land in the village.

LUIGI: Sì.

ROSINELLA: The best grapes.

LUIGI: Sì.

ROSINELLA: And he's just got the one son.

LUIGI: Mario, sì.

Pause: Luigi smug: Rosinella looks defeated: Hughie aware of the way
it has gone.

ROSINELLA: (*To Hughie*) It's looking very very bad, son. (*To Luigi:*
with disgust and sadness) That's why you wanted her back?

LUIGI: What's so wrong with you? You understand how
these things work – or are you the big lady now – think
she's too good for us still here?

ROSINELLA: (*To Hughie*) We better go, son. (*To Luigi, as they*
make to go) You're a sponger, you know that? Always were
a sponger. You sponged off my sister, you sponged off
me. You even sponged your daughter getting brought
up and now she's big, you want her married so you can
sponge off her. Your own lassie.

(*Could use 'mooch' instead.*)

LUIGI: Ciao, Ugo. (*To Rosinella*) Tell him I'm not letting Lucia
out of this house till he's back in Scotland. (*To Hughie*)
Fa attenzione al sole, eh?

Luigi turns his back on them: they go out: lights up on Lucia: she stands up, smiles expectantly: Hughie shakes his head sadly.

LUIGI: (*Voice from offstage: shouting/demanding/angry*) Lucia! Lucia! (*She runs.*)

Scene Twelve

Italy: Massimo's house

Rosinella and Hughie: Rosinella sitting, defeated: Hughie pacing, agitated.

HUGHIE: She's engaged! Engaged!

ROSINELLA: I can't believe it.

HUGHIE: Who is this guy, anyway?

ROSINELLA: No, I can believe it. I could believe anything with that one. 'His lassie. His lassie.'

HUGHIE: So what do we do now?

ROSINELLA: I don't know, son. I just don't know.

HUGHIE: I need to see Lucia.

ROSINELLA: I told you what he said.

HUGHIE: I don't care what he said. I want to see Lucia.

ROSINELLA: I told you – he says he's no letting her out the house. He means that.

HUGHIE: There must be something we can do.

ROSINELLA: I wish there was.

HUGHIE: You mean that's it? Finito?

ROSINELLA: Hughie, son ...

HUGHIE: (*Interrupting/furious/shouting*) I have waited years – YEARS – for Lucia. Blending into the background, knowing my place – 'Och it's just you, Hughie', – 'wee Hughie' – 'only Hughie' ... But I am not going back to it, do you hear me? I have not come two thousand miles to get my back blistered and my lips cracked. I have come for Lucia and I am not leaving without her.

ROSINELLA: (*Momentarily stunned/but impressed by the outburst*) Hughie ...

HUGHIE: There must be something we can do. There MUST be.

ROSINELLA: I wish I knew ...

HUGHIE: Think, Rosinella.

ROSINELLA: (*Despondent*) You heard what he said ...

HUGHIE: Think.

ROSINELLA: (*Slow realisation/rising excitement*) Maybe? ... Maybe there is something ... Could be ...

HUGHIE: What? Tell me?

ROSINELLA: Tomorrow's the feast.

HUGHIE: So?

ROSINELLA: It goes on and on and on, half the night –
drinking, singing, dancing, then the fireworks ... They'll
all be at the piazza ... All ... except ...

HUGHIE: (*Realising significance*) Lucia.

Rosinella nods.

Scene Thirteen

Night of feast: Outside Luigi's house

Bring up paesano music, noise of crowd celebrating and enjoying themselves in background. Maybe lights: celebrations going on in village square behind house.

Lucia at window: looks out to the sky and all round as though for the last time.

LUCIA: I'm sorry, daddy. But it's my life, and I've had enough of other people deciding for me. It's time to make my own choices.

She goes in.

Enter Rosinella and Hughie carrying a ladder: talking in urgent whispers.

ROSINELLA: Hurry up. Hurry up. Sshh. Ssshhh!

HUGHIE: I'm coming. Ssshhh. Sssshhhh.

ROSINELLA: Here we are. Sshh.

HUGHIE: Where?

ROSINELLA: Up there. That one.

Hughie puts the ladder up to the window.

HUGHIE: Where is she?

ROSINELLA: I told her to be ready.

HUGHIE: (*Shouts/whispers*) Lucia.

ROSINELLA: Lucia!

HUGHIE: Lucia, I've come for you.

ROSINELLA: Lucia, he's come for you.

HUGHIE: I love you, Lucia.

ROSINELLA: He says he loves you, Lucia.

HUGHIE: (*To Rosinella*) Do you mind?

ROSINELLA: What?

HUGHIE: This is, kind of – my moment – you know what I mean?

ROSINELLA: (*Slightly indignant*) Ma, it means a lot to me too, you know.

Lucia has appeared at window.

LUCIA: Hey, you two.

ROSINELLA: She's there. Look.

HUGHIE: You ready, Lucia?

LUCIA: Yes. I'll get my things.

She goes in.

Rosinella pushes Hughie up the ladder.

ROSINELLA: Right. Up you go.

Hughie takes a few steps up, then comes back down.

ROSINELLA: What?

HUGHIE: I've never done anything like this before.

ROSINELLA: I should bloody well hope no. Get up they
     steps.

Hughie takes a couple of steps up, comes back down.

HUGHIE: You're absolutely sure this will work?

ROSINELLA: That's the way it is. You keep her out for just
     one night, then you've got to marry her. Now go.

Hughie takes couple of steps up, then comes down.

HUGHIE: Could I no just do what my brother did and get
     her pregnant?

ROSINELLA: (*Really annoyed*) You love that girl or you don't
     love that girl?

HUGHIE: 'Course I do. 'Course I do.

ROSINELLA: Then get up they steps.

Hughie goes up to window: no Lucia: he leans in, looks back out.

HUGHIE: She's no there.

ROSINELLA: What do you mean she's no there?

Hughie's head disappears in again.

HUGHIE: It's that dark ... I can't see a thing ...

He climbs in, anxiously watched by Rosinella: she hears thumps and bumps, then silence.

ROSINELLA: Hughie? Hughie? Lucia? Hughie?

Nothing happening: Rosinella goes up a few steps.

ROSINELLA: Hughie? What's going on ... Hughie?

She reaches the window, leans in, looks back down, makes her decision: climbs in the window.

ROSINELLA: (*As she climbs in*) Hughie ... Lucia ... What's going on ...?

When she is in, Lucia and Hughie appear from behind the house: Lucia with a bag, mildly miffed.

LUCIA: You trying to warn the whole village? What do you want with a ladder anyway?

HUGHIE: It was Rosinella's idea.

LUCIA: That's not even my room. You might've got the room right.

They look around, see Rosinella is not there.

HUGHIE: Oh, where is she now?

LUCIA: She must've gone. Come on.

They move away.

HUGHIE: Where to?

LUCIA: Where do you think? Up a tree.

HUGHIE: What you got in the bag?

LUCIA: Stuff to keep us going. Bread, salami, cheese ...

HUGHIE: And ginger?

LUCIA: Oh yes ... Lots of ginger. Come on.

They go. Rosinella reappears at window, looks out, wondering, then sees them disappear together: she goes to call them, then realises they are on their own. They don't see her: she blows them a kiss and gives them a little wave.

Wipes away a tear: sighs sadly and leans on the windowsill looking out, longingly: in background. Music dies down, the noise reduces.

Massimo enters, wondering what is going on. He sees her but she does not see him: a smile spreads across his face. He goes to the foot of the ladder: throws up a pebble.

MASSIMO: Hey, Rosinella.

ROSINELLA: Massimo!

MASSIMO: I've come for you.

ROSINELLA: Oh Massimo, you've come for me.

MASSIMO: I love you, Rosie.

ROSINELLA: Oh, I love you too, Massimo. (*Rosinella goes coy, wicked smile*) But my daddy's locked me up … says I've not to see you …

MASSIMO: That's why I'm here. To steal you away. To take you back to Scozia.

ROSINELLA: I'm coming, Massimo.

He holds the ladder steady: she heaves herself out of window: climbs down: just as she reaches the bottom, there is a huge bang, maybe flashing lights.

Rosinella jumps.

ROSINELLA: What's that!

Massimo puts his hand on his heart, looks lovingly at her.

MASSIMO: That's ma heart, Rosie. And he's beating just for you.

They embrace: more fireworks go off, lights, etc.

THE END